Easy Calligraphy

the ABCs of hand lettering

For My Family:
Brendon, Bryon, Heather, and Dan.

No. 1778
$14.95

2132

Easy
Calligraphy
the ABCs of hand lettering

by Judy Ramsey

TAB TAB BOOKS Inc.
BLUE RIDGE SUMMIT, PA. 17214

FIRST EDITION

FIRST PRINTING

Copyright © 1984 by TAB BOOKS Inc.
Printed in the United States of America

Library of Congress Cataloging in Publication Data

Ramsey, Judy.
Easy calligraphy.

Includes index.
1. Lettering. 2. Calligraphy. I. Title.
NK3600.R35   1984   745.6'197   84-12389
ISBN 0-8306-0778-1
ISBN 0-8306-1778-7 (pbk.)

Contents

Acknowledgments

I have called upon numerous sources in attempting to make calligraphy as easy as possible. I would like to acknowledge and thank the most prominent of these sources: The Society for Italic Handwriting; Faber-Castell Corporation, makers of Higgins Inks; Vemco Corporation; Sheaffer Eaton Division of Textron, Inc.; Wing K. Leong of the Chinese Art Studio, Portland, Oregon; Dover Publications for permission to reprint illustrations from "Exotic Alphabets and Ornaments" by William Rowe and "Calligraphic Alphabets" by Arthur Baker; Vearl Blackwell of Clauson's, Vancouver, Washington; Linda Kelso for photographic contributions and professional assistance; Nancy Richards for helpful preliminary work on this book; and especially to professional calligrapher Aleta Kelso for supplying sample exercises and numerous examples of easy calligraphy.

Introduction

Everyone admires beautiful and decorative hand-writing, or *calligraphy;* yet most people think they have to be an artist to write like one. Calligraphy can, however, be easy to learn and use.

Easy Calligraphy: The ABCs of Hand Lettering is a highly illustrated book that can show you how to write like an artist with smooth, flowing letters that are both readable and enjoyable. You will learn my simplified approach to calligraphy which takes you step-by-step from choosing the correct materials through planning and actually producing artistic name tags, place cards, certificates, business cards, signs, and personal letters for fun and profit. Best of all, you'll be graphically guided each step of the way by more than 160 clear illustrations of alphabets, strokes, letters, methods, and materials.

You'll learn how to make practicing easy and fun, how to select inexpensive pens and papers, how to make your own calligraphy pen, how to plan calligraphy products, and how to set up a professional calligraphy studio and make extra money with your new skill.

The self-study lesson plans and dozens of easy exercises will help you develop these skills easily and quickly with clear examples and lots of help. The comprehensive Glossary offers easy definitions of more than 100 words you will learn as a calligrapher.

Whether you are a professional calligrapher, an artist, a graphic designer, or someone who simply wants to improve your penmanship, you'll profit from learning easy calligraphy.

1.
Getting Started in Calligraphy

Calligraphy is the art of beautiful writing. It is an art form that can be learned. By mastering a series of basic pen strokes you can become one of those people whose handwriting is admired: a calligrapher. All it takes is patient practice and a few inexpensive tools and materials.

The beginnings of calligraphy can be traced to the beginning of recorded history. The term calligraphy comes from the Greek *kalos,* meaning beautiful and *graphos,* meaning writing.

Your study of calligraphy can accomplish many goals. You can study calligraphy simply to improve your everyday handwriting, or you can use your new skills at home or on the job to produce beautiful, personalized invitations or other forms of communication. More intense study and practice, may lead to a part- or full-time business.

As you begin your study of calligraphy, become aware of the many places where calligraphy is used. Several advertisements in your morning newspaper probably incorporate this form of beautiful writing. As you drive to work, notice the billboards and store front signs that are lettered in calligraphy. In your daily mail, several letterheads may have been designed by a calligrapher, as may the business card someone hands you during the day.

Calligraphy can be used to design uniquely personal invitations, announcements, awards, or placecards for a special dinner. Posters, book jackets, and package labels are also sometimes written in calligraphy.

A popular use for calligraphy is beautifully lettering a favorite quotation in an appropriate style and framing it for use as a wall hanging. This project can be done for your own home or for a gift for a special friend or relative.

The relatively simple, yet functional and beautiful, Italic modes of calligraphic writing are suitable for use in all your writing. Italic writing is easy to read because of its clean lines. Personal correspondence, notes, bulletins, and any other written communication can comfortably be done in Italic handwriting.

BEGINNING TOOLS AND MATERIALS

As your study of calligraphy progresses you will want, and need, more sophisticated tools and materials, perhaps eventually using a professional calligrapher's pen and expensive, special papers. But what you need to get started is inexpensive and easy to find. Beginning pens and papers can come from an art, stationery, or possibly even a variety store.

The recommended pen for the first section of this book is a chisel-tip felt pen (Fig. 1-1). The chisel-tip felt pen has a tip that is similar to the nib,

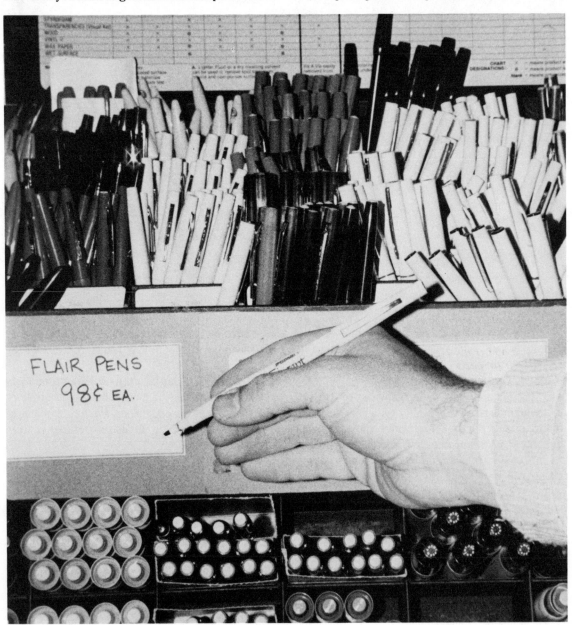

Fig. 1-1. A typical felt pen.

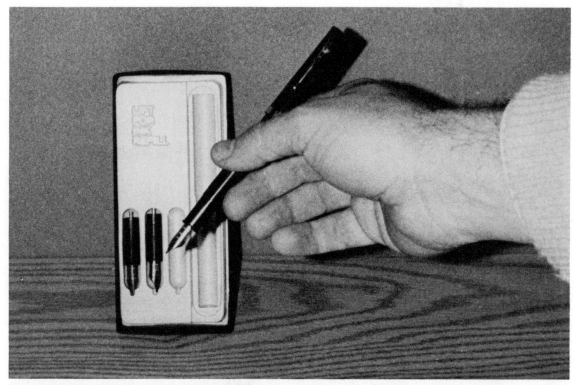

Fig. 1-2. This type of fountain pen uses ink cartridges.

or tip, of the true calligraphy pen, but is much easier to use. Two good chisel tip pens are the Eberhard-Faber "Design" #492 Chisel Point pen and the "Chiz'1" AD marker.

The chisel-tip calligraphy pen is a good choice to use until you have become familiar with the letter forms and this new style of pen. To help familiarize yourself with the calligraphy pen's characteristics carry one of your chisel-tip pens with you and use it everywhere that you write.

An alternative to the chisel-tip pen is the common, fine-point, nylon-tip pen, such as those made by Flair or Parker. The advantage of the nylon-tip pen is the smooth stroke that can be an aid in the learning process. Some students prefer to begin directly with a calligraphic fountain pen (Figs. 1-2 and 1-3). These will be discussed in Chapter 5. Ballpoint pens neither feel nor write like calligraphy pens; they are, therefore, unsuitable for the practice of calligraphy lettering.

To make your chisel-tip pen or nylon-tip pen

last longer, be sure to keep it tightly capped whenever it is not in use. To renew a ragged chisel-tip pen, shave the fibers off the flat side with a very sharp razor blade. Be sure not to alter the width of the point.

A variety of inexpensive papers are available on which to practice your calligraphy. One of the best is lined notebook paper. Standard notebook paper is 8½ × 11 inches with ruled lines 5/16 inch apart, a good width for most calligraphy exercises. The paper is also thin enough to use for tracing exercises.

Another good choice for practice paper is duplicator paper, which can be purchased at any office supply store. It is least expensive by the ream.

Graph paper is also used by many student calligraphers. It should be the type with ¼-inch squares. The advantage of graph paper is that it allows you to more easily see the proportions of the strokes and letters you are practicing.

You may find onion skin or tracing paper a

Fig. 1-3. Calligraphy starter sets can also be purchased.

helpful aid in exercises which require tracing from the book. Onion skin is more translucent than most papers; it permits the page below to show through clearly for easy tracing.

As you can see, many inexpensive papers are available to use to practice calligraphy. Actually, any paper that will accept ink is usable. The choice is yours. Whatever paper you choose, remember to use just one side so that it is easy to read and evaluate your work.

Other than pens and paper, your beginning material needs are minimal. Keep sharp Number 2 pencils and a pencil sharpener handy. If you choose to begin with a calligraphic fountain pen, you will also want a desk blotter or several newspapers to protect your writing surface.

The professional calligrapher often requires a drafting table to do his highest quality work. As a beginner, however, there is probably an adequate writing surface in your home right now that will serve your needs (Fig. 1-4). If available, a drawing board of at least 20 by 26 inches makes an excellent calligrapher's writing surface. The slanted surface helps to create the ideal lettering position. A slanted board can be used to simulate a drawing board.

Another good writing surface is a student desk. Whatever writing surface you use should be clean and free of scars or blemishes. If a drawing board or student desk is not at your disposal, any desk or table can be used.

The height of your writing surface is also important. It should be adjusted so that your shoulders are level, in a comfortable sitting position.

Good lighting is vital. You must be able to see your work clearly, without shadows or glare. Good lighting will also help to avoid eyestrain while you are concentrating. The best source of lighting is daylight coming from the left side. When daylight is not usable, resort to a lamp with a 75- or 100-watt bulb. The lamp should be positioned so that the light comes over your left shoulder to cause the least amount of shadow on your work.

ITALIC WRITING

This book will focus on two forms of Italic writing. They are *Calligraphic,* or *Practical, Italic* (Fig. 1-5) and *Chancery Cursive.* Italic lettering is

Fig. 1-4. Any large, hard surface can be an adequate writing surface for calligraphy.

Fig. 1-5. Practical Italic.

the most popular style of calligraphy. It is suitable for a great variety of projects, and it is the calligraphic style that will most influence your current handwriting. The popularity of Italic lettering is probably due to its blend of beauty and readability.

The Italic form of calligraphy is one of the five major historic hands. Italic, Roman, Celtic, Gothic, and Bookhand each endured as the "true" alphabetic form for more than 200 years. There are numerous other styles and variations of styles from which a calligrapher can choose. Most, however, are basically grounded in one of the five major historic styles.

The Italic hand probably evolved when the Humanist or Renaissance, movement began in Italy during the fourteenth century. It appears to be an outgrowth of rapid writing with the humanistic letters.

Currently, Italic denotes slanted, connected writing that is clear and simple enough to use for all types of writing. Cursive simply means that the letters are connected.

Practical Italics and Chancery Cursive share many letter characteristics. Practical Italics is best suited to everyday writing, while Chancery Cursive presents a style appropriate to more formal occasions.

Practical Italics is an efficient, easy-to-learn hand. Italic letters are oval, with long ascenders and descenders, extending the tops and bottoms of the letters. The letters slant slightly, about 10 degrees, to the right. The direct links between letters make the style efficient, easily read, and quick to write.

Chancery Cursive, considered by many calligraphers to be the most beautiful Italic style, basically adds flourishes to the Practical Italics. Ascenders and descenders are enhanced with serifs.

The Italic hand is the most versatile style for casual and formal communication without departing from one basic form. The Italic form also allows enough flexibility to develop personal characteristics in your handwriting.

SITTING AT YOUR DESK

It's time to sit down at your calligraphy desk.

Fig. 1-6. First, assemble all your materials.

First, assemble all your materials and place them on your writing surface (Fig. 1-6). Then place your chair at about a 30-degree angle to the desk and sit so that your entire body faces toward the left. If you are using a desk with an attached seat, turn yourself at a 30-degree angle to the writing surface.

Sit erectly, but not stiffly. Put your feet comfortably under the table or desk. If you like, prop your left foot on the chair rung. It is very important to be comfortable. You will be able to work longer without fatigue if you learn early to make yourself comfortable and yet be in the proper writing position.

The proper working position will be reflected in your success in forming the strokes of calligraphic letters. Your shoulders should be level and your eyes no less than 10 inches from the paper.

You must also be relaxed in order to perform your best. If you become tense, stop and relax. Get up and walk about, even take a short stroll outside. Do a few relaxation exercises. Tighten and relax your shoulders, arms, hands and fingers. Stretch all over, then sit back down, all relaxed and ready to concentrate again.

Now, with a stack of several sheets of practice paper in front of you, it's time to pick up your pen. The way you hold the pen will be partly determined by the type of pen you have chosen as your initial tool.

If you are using the recommended chisel-tip pen, you will be using it as you will ultimately use your true calligraphy pen. With the end of the pen resting on the middle finger, hold the pen lightly between the thumb and forefinger. The pen shaft should rest between the base of the thumb and the base of the forefinger. Keep the forefinger slightly arched while writing so that the blood flows freely, keeping the finger from feeling numb. Your elbow

Fig. 1-7. Hold the pen lightly between the thumb and forefinger.

Fig. 1-8. Pull the pen toward you from top to bottom . . .

must be held out, away from the body in order to maintain the necessary 45-degree pen angle. The pen must be at a 45-degree angle for the ink to flow correctly onto the paper. See Fig. 1-17.

If you have chosen the nylon-tip pen, hold it as you would a pencil. Grip it lightly between thumb and forefinger. The lower part of the pen will rest on the middle finger.

If you are starting with a calligraphic fountain pen, it will work like a regular fountain pen, except that the ink will not flow correctly when you push the pen stroke. You must pull the pen toward you from top to bottom and from left to right (Figs. 1-8 and 1-9). The pen will only allow ink to flow when the nib, or point, is at the 45-degree angle to the paper. If you begin with a calligraphic fountain pen, be sure to use the wide nib.

Now write a few lines in your regular handwriting with whichever pen you have chosen. Your fingers and wrist move a lot, but there is probably little arm or shoulder movement.

In calligraphic writing, movement will come from the arm and shoulder; your wrist and hand will not control the pen movement. Your arm and shoulder will move the forearm, which will direct the pen across the page.

In order to maintain correct stroke and letter proportions, your effective working span is limited to about 5 inches (Fig. 1-10). When it is necessary to exceed this span, move the paper rather than the arm, whether you need to move side to side or down the page (Figs. 1-11 through 1-13). Use your left hand, which should be resting lightly on the writing surface to provide support, for moving the paper (Fig. 1-14).

After just a short time, the initial awkwardness of the unfamiliar tools will disappear and you will discover that it is less tiring to move your shoulder and arm than it is to write with all the action coming from the fingers and wrist.

Be sure to wash your hands before beginning on your calligraphy and wash frequently while practicing. When you wash, end with a cold rinse to relax your hands. Remove any jewelry which could get in your way.

Concentration is important in any learning

Fig. 1-9. . . . and from left to right.

Fig. 1-10. Your working span is limited to about five inches.

Fig. 1-11. Beginning a new letter.

Fig. 1-12. Ending the letter.

Fig. 1-13. Move the paper rather than your hand.

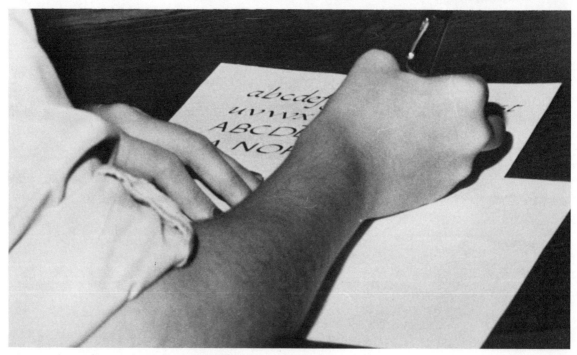

Fig. 1-14. Your left hand should be resting lightly on the writing surface.

12

situation. Locate your calligraphy table or desk where you will have the least distractions. A separate room is ideal, but a quiet corner of the bedroom, living room, or even the kitchen is adequate.

GETTING STARTED

When you begin your study of calligraphy you will be anxious to see rapid progress. You probably will. Your handwriting will improve rapidly; you will quickly become comfortable with your new pen, and you will aquire an understanding of the theory of calligraphic lettering. Don't rush yourself though. Everyone learns at his own pace. Allow yourself plenty of time to thoroughly understand and master each exercise before you move on.

A good way to watch your progress is by saving typical writing samples. Keep a couple of samples of your writing from before you began to learn calligraphy. Throughout your studies keep samples of exercises you did at various times. When you begin to use your calligraphy on personal projects, be sure to save some for future comparison. You will be able to watch your skills grow, and very soon you will begin to get those compliments on your handwriting.

Loosening-Up Exercises

The following exercises can be of use to you throughout your efforts as a calligrapher. They can serve to check your pen angle as well as help you to relax and ease into the mood for your calligraphy practice.

Exercie 1. This exercise will show you if you are holding your calligraphy pen at the correct 45-degree angle (Fig. 1-15). If you are, the up strokes will be thin, and the down strokes wide. Do several lines of this exercise, until your lines become consistent and you are sure your pen angle is right. Either lined notebook paper or graph paper is best for all these exercises.

Exercise 2. Make several of these long and short strokes shown in Fig. 1-16. Do yours look just like the example? The points at the top and bottom of each stroke also indicate a correct 45-degree pen angle. If your lines do not have points at both top

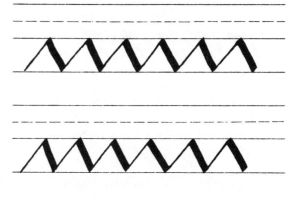

Fig. 1-15. Exercise 1: hold your pen at a 45-degree angle.

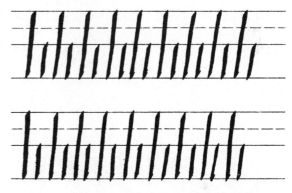

Fig. 1-16. Exercise 2: This exercise also requires a correct pen angle.

and bottom, return to Exercise 1 and repeat several more rows. Then come back to this exercise and make several more long and short strokes. If they now have points at the top and bottom, your pen is at the best angle. The entire point of the pen nib should touch the paper at all times.

Exercise 3. Make a number of triangles by starting at the upper right corner, pushing the pen left to the upper left corner, coming straight down to the next line on the paper, and ending with a line back up to the upper right hand corner (Fig. 1-17). Your thin and wide lines should be in the same places as those in the example. If they are not, return to Exercises 1 and 2 for more practice before moving on.

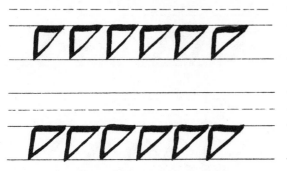

Fig. 1-17. Exercise 3: make a number of triangles.

Fig. 1-19. Exercise 5: equal spacing.

Exercise 4. These strokes must be kept parallel at about a 10-degree slant to the right (Fig. 1-18). Start with a down stroke, making sure that both top and bottom points touch the lines of your practice paper. Consistency is a vital factor in calligraphy. Practice this exercise until you can do a line rapidly and keep it in proportion. The strokes on lines above and below should nearly touch each other.

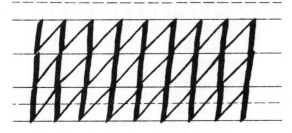

Fig. 1-18. Exercise 4: keep the strokes parallel and angled at 10 degrees.

Exercise 5. Beginning at the lower edge, make a few rows of the diagonal lines shown in Fig. 1-19. Equal spacing is your goal.

Exercise 6. As your last loosening up exercise, do a number of rows of the continuous "e" shapes shown in Fig. 1-20. Relax your hand and remember that movement should come from your shoulder and arm, not your hand and fingers.

After you complete these exercises, you will

Fig. 1-20. Exercise 6: continuous "e" shapes.

begin to see how your calligraphy pen functions, creating the thick and thin lines that give calligraphy letters their distinctive appearance.

If you feel comfortable with your pen and the results of your first exercises, you are ready to begin learning the basic calligraphy strokes. If not, return to the exercises and repeat them again. All of the exercises can first be traced from the examples in this book and then drawn freehand. Anytime you sit down to work with your calligraphy, do a few rows of each exercise.

Practice, Practice, Practice

The best way to make sure that you will learn any new skill is to practice faithfully; this is especially true with calligraphy. You must train your arm and shoulder to do the work of writing. It will take a great deal of concentration and repeated efforts. Remain on guard that your fingers and wrist do not automatically take over the task of forming letters and moving across the page.

Practice for at least 20 minutes each day would be the optimum practice schedule. If you cannot set such a schedule, however, create the best practice schedule you can and stick to it. If you can only practice three times each week, make the time productive. You will still learn a great deal and progress with your calligraphy skills quickly. Try to get into a routine of practicing at the same time and in the same place each day.

Stay as faithful as possible to your practice schedule, but don't attempt to keep working when you are overtired. Your concentration will not last, and you will become discouraged.

Your patient practice will be rewarded by a rapid learning of the theory of calligraphy and a quick building of your skills. Remember that regular practice will do more to improve your handwriting than will raw talent.

A Typical Practice Session

You will soon discover your own best practice routine. Following is a suggested practice session that works for many students.

- Relax. Your practice will be most productive if you begin with a relaxed attitude. If necessary do a few relaxation exercises before beginning, or do whatever activity helps you to relax—take a bath, walk the dog, or read a chapter in a good mystery novel.
- Assemble your tools. If you keep all your calligraphy tools and materials together near your practice place this will be an easy task. For a while all you will need is your calligraphy pen, several sheets of practice paper, and this book. As you progress you will want to add more tools and materials.
- Seat yourself at your desk or table (Fig. 1-21 and 1-22). Check yourself for the correct calligrapher's posture. You should be at approximately a 30-degree angle to your writing surface, sitting comfortably erect. Hold your pen lightly between thumb and forefinger with the pen shaft resting between the base of the two and your forefinger slightly arched. Your elbow must be held away from your body to ensure the necessary 45-

degree angle between pen and paper.

- Warm up with the loosening-up exercises described earlier in this chapter. These exercises will check your pen angle and focus your mind on calligraphy.
- Review your recent work. Refresh your mind by reviewing your most recently developed calligraphy knowledge. Quickly run through any new material you encountered in your most recent practice session. A short practice session on review material will build naturally into a productive learning session.
- Tackle some new material. When you are comfortable about yesterday's practice material, move on to the next area. Read carefully and study any examples or exercises. Trace new strokes and letters if it will help you to understand how they are formed. Then draw the strokes. Draw each new stroke until it begins to feel easy and fluent. Do not hurry any step. Your skills will build most quickly if you spend enough time on each new concept or exercise to learn it thoroughly.
- Evaluate your work. When you stop for the day, look back at your work. You should be pleased at the rapid development of your calligraphy skills.
- Clean up. Get into the habit of putting all your tools and materials away at the end of a practice session. It's much easier now than at the beginning of tomorrow's study time. If you later use a professional calligrapher's pen, it will be vital to clean it after any use.

Hints for Left-Handers

If you are lefthanded, learning calligraphy may be difficult. It will take some adjustments, but it can be done. Some suggestions may be helpful.

You must reverse the seating and positioning directions already given. Experiment with paper positions to achieve the 45-degree angle between pen nib and paper. Depending on what works best for you, you may be able to use a regular right-handed pen, or you may need to purchase a special left-handed pen. Left-handed pens are readily available at most stores that carry calligraphy supplies. You may have more trouble adjusting to your pen,

Fig. 1-21. Small drafting tables make good calligraphy desks.

Fig. 1-22. Make sure that your desk has sufficient light.

but if you relax and keep trying, the adjustment will come. Do not grip the pen too tightly.

In most cases you can simply substitute "right" for "left" and "left" for "right" and continue with the exercises as directed. For some letters, however, you must reverse the direction of the stroke. You will learn which strokes must be reversed, as you become more familiar with your pen and its functioning.

Take care not to smear the ink with your hand as you letter from left to right. With a little extra work, you can become a successful left-handed calligrapher.

MAKE IT FUN

It's fun to learn a new skill, and it's fun to watch that new skill grow. Calligraphy is a skill that grows rapidly with faithful, but not rigorous, practice.

As you become more adept at calligraphy use it anywhere you write: to take notes, to write a letter, to copy a recipe. In just a few weeks you can be lettering special projects to decorate your home and to give as treasured gifts.

Calligraphy is an art that is open to everyone. It's easy to learn a few basic calligraphy styles and use them. It's also an inexpensive craft. The cost of beginning supplies is minimal: just a practice pen or two and some paper. Everything else you will need to get started is probably in your home or office already: good lighting and a comfortable writing surface and chair.

Calligraphy is an ancient art. It's beginnings can be traced back to very early civilization. In order to appreciate the history that has culminated in such an attractive craft, let's take time to explore the beginning and subsequent developments of the art. Chapter 2 will sketch a history of calligraphy, discuss major changes and historical influences, and introduce the five most important calligraphy styles through the ages.

While taking the time to learn a little about the background of calligraphy, take a few moments every day and practice the warm-up exercises. Be sure to check your pen angle often.

Relax, take your time, practice faithfully, and calligraphy will be both fun and easy.

2.

Calligraphy
Through the Ages

The earliest written communication was through pictures. Even before pictographs were used, however, each primitive culture had a form of silent communication. Some included the use of stone mementos, sticks as account sheets, and knotted strings.

Eventually pictographs evolved into symbols for sounds. which were combined to make words. These phonograms were designed by the Egyptians, who failed, however, to make the last step to a phonetic alphabet.

It is not clear who took that step to the phonetic alphabet. It was, however, probably the most important advancement in the history of writing. It laid the groundwork for all written communication since that time.

A HISTORY OF CALLIGRAPHIC LETTERS

The beginnings of the alphabet we use in the western world today are based on the Greek alphabet. Even the term *alphabet* comes from the two first letters of the Greek alphabet, *alpha* and *beta*.

The origin of the Greek alphabet is controversial, but one accepted theory is that it came from the Phoenician alphabet consisting of 22 letters and dating back to around 1600 B.C. Indications are that the Greeks adopted the Phoenician alphabet before 1000 B.C. and by 403 B.C. had revised it into an alphabet of 24 formal letters. This Greek alphabet proved suitable for all the Indo-European languages and established the course of western writing.

The Romans used the Greek alphabet and made modifications that brought the alphabet to the form that we now recognize and use. The Romans added two new letters, revised eight, and accepted 13 as they appeared in the Greek. The 23-letter alphabet comprised what became known as the classic Roman alphabet and was sufficient for writing Latin. The letters J, U, and W did not appear in the early Roman alphabet; they were added in the tenth, twelfth, and fifteenth centuries.

The Romans are also credited with changing the names of the letters from the alpha, beta, gamma, etc., to the A, B, C sounds that we currently employ. In addition, the Romans perfected the letterforms, resulting in the still-famous inscription in the base of the Trajan column in Rome, carved around the year 114 A.D. Those beautifully designed and created letters represent centuries of development in the art of writing and have influenced all western writing since their execution.

Earliest Minuscule Alphabet

The first minuscule, or lower case, alphabet was developed long after the standard Classic Roman Capitals were accepted throughout the civilized western world. Many styles of writing, based on the Roman alphabet, were popular for a short time, but it was not until the seventh or eighth century that *minuscules,* or lower case letters, came into use.

Little information is available about the beginnings of minuscules. How or where they were created and first used is unclear. Some evidence indicates that this alphabet developed from a specific type of documentary hand used during the eighth century. It is likely that the monastery in Constantinople played an important part in its early development.

The documentary-hand that employed the first minuscules is referred to as *Carolingian,* or *Carlovingian,* after the Frankish dynasty of Carl the Great. While the origin of the minuscule is vague, the reasons for its instigation and popularity are apparent. War-induced poverty coincided with a shortage of papyrus following the Arab conquest of Egypt during the seventh century. The use of minuscules reduced the cost of using the more expensive vellum. A quick, informal style of writing was becoming necessary; the revival of learning when peace was restored in the ninth century caused a need for scholarly textbooks.

The first minuscules were even and of a uniform size (Fig. 2-1). Letters were joined or not according to strict rules. There was no division between words. Ascenders and descenders are emphatic. Carolingian did not employ majuscules as such.

Carolingian, adopted by Charlemagne, represented the first attempt to establish a standard hand for all of western Europe since the fall of the Roman Empire. Carolingian is an historically important hand also because it was the inspiration for the humanistic writing of the 15th century, which is the basis of the lower case Roman letters used today.

Carolingian reigned as the dominant handwriting style in Europe from the ninth to the eleventh centuries, when Gothic began to take over.

The Five Major Historic Hands

Each of five basic historic hands was a dominant lettering style for at least 200 years, considered by scribes and readers of its day as the "true form" of the alphabet. Many other styles of calligraphy have existed throughout history, but these five were most enduring. We will look at each of these handwriting styles, but our focus will be on Italic, the most popular form of calligraphy, as well as the most practical for everyday use.

The five major historic styles of calligraphy

Fig. 2-1. Early minuscules.

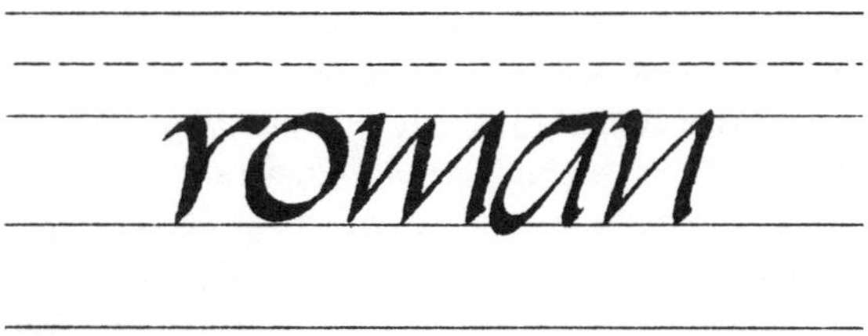

Roman

Fig. 2-2. Roman hand.

include Roman, Celtic, Gothic, Italic, and Bookhand. Following is a look at the characteristics and historic significance of each hand.

Roman. The historic significance of the Roman alphabet has already been discussed. Our alphabet comes directly from the Roman (Fig. 2-2).

Classic Roman handwriting has influenced lettering, as well as contemporary typography, for nearly 2,000 years. The Roman hand consists entirely of majuscules, but can be successfully combined with Bookhand minuscules.

Each Roman capital has a personality of its own, and a great deal of practice is required to produce acceptable Roman letters. It is probably the most difficult alphabet to learn, even though it is the most familiar. Each letter has its own identity, and the style cannot be described in a few sentences.

The unifying factor of the Roman hand is the proportion of each letter and its relationship to other letters. The letters stand firmly and evenly on the base line. The writer's pen angle must change with some letters in order to produce the correct stroke width. Roman letters are clear and simple; the style communicates well.

A broad-tip pen cannot exactly reproduce the precision and beauty of the chisel cuts in the Trajan column, but with much diligent practice a reasonable facsimile can be achieved.

While Roman capitals were historically used for inscription, a pen version called *quadrata* appeared. A square-cut reed or quill was used as a pen. Since the quadrata required painstaking detail to each letter, it soon gave way to another variation, called *rustica*. Rustica was a freely written, elegant form of lettering, characterized by thin upright strokes and thick cross strokes.

Rustica was in turn replaced by a style of lettering called *uncial,* so named because they were an *uncia,* or a Roman inch, in height. Later uncials lost the uniformity of height. The unicial style consisted of freely written, rounded majuscules.

All of these Roman styles of lettering are used still by professional calligraphers.

Celtic. When Christianity was introduced into Ireland during the fifth century, texts written in quadrata were distributed. In copying the scriptures, the Celts used the quadrata form, but they added their own touches and decorations. The letters became even more rounded, and by the ninth century the style had become extremely creative.

Celtic scribes also began to incorporate *runes,* pre-Roman native letters of the British Isles, Scandinavia, and northern Europe. Runes were once used as magic signs and pagan symbols, and then were organized into an alphabet. These runes were made of straight lines, and the Celts imposed their outlines on the Roman letters, creating a new alphabet suitable for abstract ornament.

The Celtic alphabet (Fig. 2-3) contains a number of alternate letter forms that are unified by bulging letters and the unusual Celtic serif. Celtic letters consist of a letter-height to pen-width ratio of about five to one, as compared to the Roman ratio of about eight to one. This makes the Celtic letters appear much heavier than the Roman. A flatter pen angle, about 15 degrees, creates an alphabet rounder and fatter than Roman.

Celtic letters allow each calligrapher to develop his own personal Celtic style. The choice of a thick or thin pen determines either heavy or light letters. Celtic letters can be either simple and clean or complex and ornamental. The choice of spacing creates either an open or crowded appearance.

Fig. 2-3. Celtic hand.

Fig. 2-4. Gothic hand.

Many Celtic letters have as many as six alternate forms. Celtic letters can also be squeezed or expanded to fill the necessary space. The letters can even overlap without losing readability.

Celtic lettering can be fun. It is most suitable for optimistic, happy quotations or other bright writing. Celtic calligraphy is a style that encourages, even demands, that the calligrapher's personality shine through. It is a style to enjoy.

Gothic. The Gothic influence on lettering began during the twelfth century. The Gothic style (Fig. 2-4) was the first to employ a combination of majuscules and minuscules. Gothic lettering flourished for more than 300 years. Parchment and vellum were scarce during the time the Gothic hand was popular; partially the reason for its popularity was its condensed style, which allows a great deal of copy to be written in a small space.

The Gothic style is used today primarily on formal presentations such as diplomas and certificates, and for mastheads.

Gothic lettering, properly called *Textur* or *Textura* because of its even patterning, reached the peak of its popularity during the fifteenth century. Italy was already moving heavily into a revival of the Roman calligraphy.

The ornate, difficult to read, Gothic form of lettering is deceptive; the style is not difficult to learn. The main objective is to keep the black strokes and the white spaces exactly equal. The style evolved from a combining of the Roman Rustica and the runic capitals from the Celtic hand.

Spacing between words is one letter wide; spacing between lines is one letter high.

Gothic lettering consists of one basic shape: the box. The calligrapher's challenge is to create all the letters of the alphabet with that one basic shape. A 30-degree pen angle is required for lettering.

Gothic capitals are often incorporated into pictures that help describe the text. This was especially important when Gothic lettering was dominant because few people at that time could read.

Bookhand. During the fifteenth century, Italy rediscovered Carolingian writing, which Charlemagne had made prominent several centuries earlier. The Italians mistakenly thought the many available Carolingian manuscripts represented an ancient Roman hand. *Bookhand,* (Fig. 2-5) or Humanist Bookhand, is the script that fifteenth century Italian scribes created through the modification of Carolingian letters, which were originally based on the Classic Roman hand.

Because paper was more readily available and less expensive than in earlier centuries, scholars were able to expand the letter sizes and develop a more open countenance. Type for the earliest printing presses was adapted from the Italian Bookhand style.

Bookhand is a familiar letter form today both because it is still in use and has been for several hundred years, and because it resembles Roman minuscules. An easy to read style, Bookhand functions well in size. Bookhand is a simple, disciplined style that can employ serifs if desired. A 30-degree angle is used to pen Bookhand letters.

Italic. Italic writing changed the entire concept of calligraphy. Prior to Italics, calligraphy had been restricted to monastic scribes and professional copyists. With the beginning of Italic writing, calligraphy became available to a much larger portion of the population. Scientists, politicians, ar-

Fig. 2-5. Bookhand.

Fig. 2-6. Italic hand.

tists, and law clerks, among others, became involved in calligraphy.

The Italic form (Fig. 2-6) was probably a natural consequence of writing the Humanist Bookhand style quickly. Italic letters represent the first time that both the formal court and the vernacular shared a common writing style that could be widely read. Michelangelo and Petrarch were expert Italic calligraphers.

Italic writing is characterized by a slight slant to the right. The pen must be at a 45-degree angle to the paper. Letters are oval in shape and usually five pen widths high.

The most popular calligraphic lettering style today is Italic. Within the Italic category several lettering variations exist. Among them are Chancery Cursive, Formal Italic, and Straight, or Practical, Italic. This book will fully explore Chancery

Fig. 2-7. Early ornate hand.

Cursive as a special handwriting, and Straight or Practical Italic as a casual, or everyday, handwriting style.

History has preserved a variety of handwriting styles (Fig. 2-7). Those listed above are the most enduring and the most important for a beginning calligraphy student to identify.

The art of fine writing has had to survive many devastating periods of history. As did many other things, calligraphy nearly disappeared during the Medieval Ages, roughly from the time of the fall of the Roman Empire in 476 A.D. until about the end of the fifteenth century. Poverty was often a way of life, and writing materials and tools were usually expensive and scarce. Civilization was generally ruder than classical or present times, and secular development was not often encouraged.

Scribes of the Middle Ages were mainly concerned with preserving the Word of God. Many scholarly works from classical times were lost.

It was not until the Renaissance, which was initiated early in the fourteenth century, that an intellectual movement began a revival of letters and art that marked the transition from medieval to modern history. This revival of learning, sparked by Italian poets Dante, Alighieri and Petrarch, led to a renewed interest in classical Greek and Roman literature. With this new desire for literature and learning, a natural increase in the demand for book production was seen.

The invention of movable type and the introduction to Europe of the Oriental papermaking technique allowed printing to replace the majority of handwriting in book making. Even though a quest for knowledge existed, therefore, the need for expert calligraphers declined. The art of calligraphy practically ceased.

The Arts and Crafts Movement in England

In England at the end of the nineteenth century a revolt against the mechanization of life, known as the Arts and Crafts Movement, began. About 1870 an English writer and artist focused attention on the nearly extinct art of fine writing; calligraphy.

Morris studied the work of ancient scribes and

Fig. 2-8. An illuminated letter.

experimented with pen on parchment to attempt to achieve the same results. He wrote and illuminated many texts in Humanistic and medieval fashion (Fig. 2-8); then he began a study of fifteenth century printing.

His efforts led papermakers and ink suppliers, as well as others, to strive for long-forgotten standards. An early convert was Edward Johnston, who abandoned his medical studies to become a scribe. Johnston rediscovered the craft of cutting and sharpening reeds and quills, how to use the pens, and how to make manuscripts (Figs. 2-9 and 2-10).

In 1899 Johnston began to teach at the Central School of Arts and Crafts and later at the Royal College of Art. Among his first students were several who became influential calligraphers and designers of lettering. In 1906 Johnston published a 500-page book on lettering which found its way to Germany in 1910, where it supported the independent work of artists there.

Art schools throughout Europe followed the lead of the Royal College of Art by offering courses in lettering and writing. The design of typography passed from the hands of engineers into the hands of artists and craftsmen specializing in calligraphy.

The Revival of Calligraphy in the United States

The revival of calligraphy in the United States was about 10 years behind the Arts and Crafts Movement of Europe. If 1902 Frank Chouteau Brown authored a book titled *Letters and Lettering:*

ITALIC HANDWRITING as practised today is a simplified traditional system which derives from the Italian Renaissance. The revival has become so widely established that this Society is now represented in many countries & is continuously expanding as the virtues of the script become known. The versions of today belong completely to our time & circumstances. The legibility & beauty of italic handwriting & the speed at which it can be written without falling into decay are its qualities.

Fig. 2-9. Hand from the Society for Italic Handwriting.

It would be interesting to learn what effect members' handwriting has had upon other people. For instance, back in the early fifties, I had to do business with a stonemason: with his receipt was a note complimenting me on the clarity of my writing.
A firm from which I purchased a garage wrote to say that my letter had been placed on the notice board as an example to the office staff.

Fig. 2-10. Sample hand of an SIH member.

A Treatise with 200 Examples.

In his volume Brown praised Morris for initiating a revival of calligraphy, but pointed out a need for more classical balance. Brown gave generous space in his book to Italics, which he felt Morris had neglected.

In London in 1921 the Society of Scribes and Illuminators, "zealously directed toward the production of books and documents by hand," was formed. During the 1930s, exhibits of the group appeared in five American cities. In 1952, recognizing the surge of interest in Italic writing; the organization established the Society for Italic Handwriting, which quickly drew an international membership (Figs. 2-11 through 2-14).

Throughout the United States individuals and groups have promoted calligraphy as a craft that others besides artists can learn. Calligraphy classes are now available in most areas at a reasonable cost.

East Asian Calligraphy

Western calligraphy has become an art that anyone can master with practice. In China, Korea and Japan, however, calligraphy is considered a true art form, equal to painting. Calligraphy for all three cultures derives from the written form of Chinese.

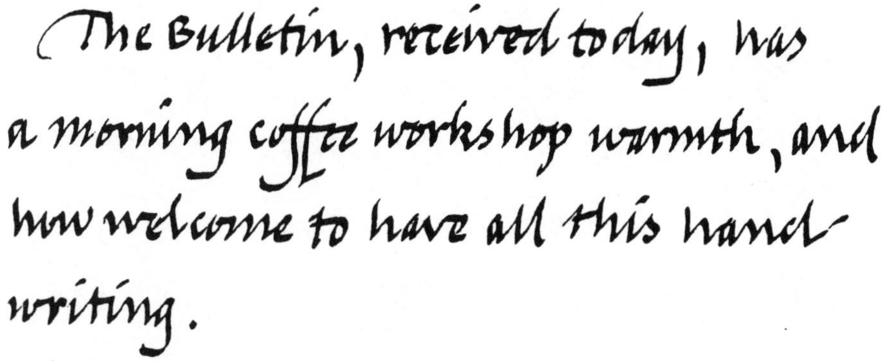

Fig. 2-11. An ornate italic sample.

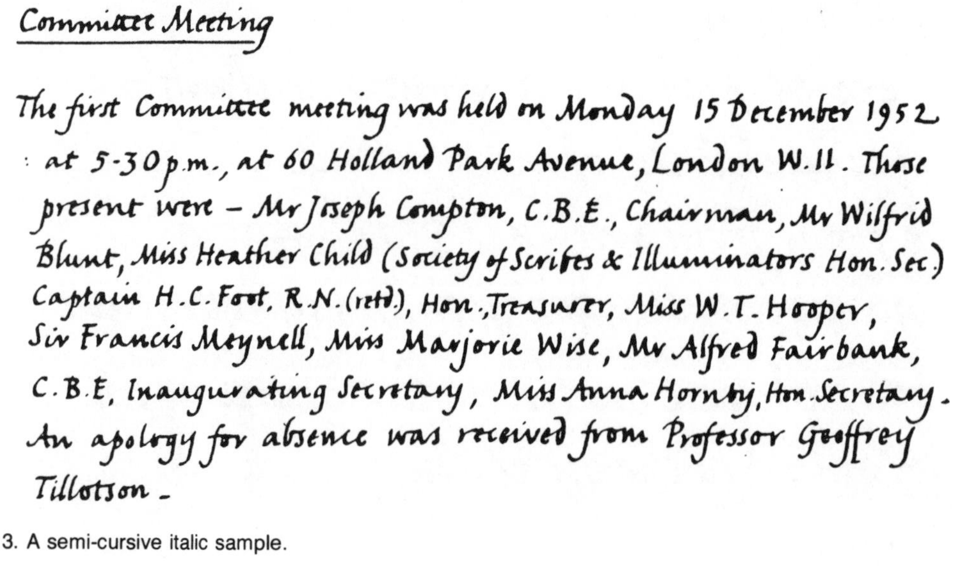

Fig. 2-13. A semi-cursive italic sample.

Clive Wilkinson is one of three new committee members. He is Headmaster of The Colleton County Primary School, Twyford, Berkshire. The others are Brother William Sherwood, mentioned in the Secretary's Notes; and Brenda Berman who teaches calligraphy at City and Guilds of London School of Art.

Fig. 2-13. A beautiful example of applied italics.

Early Chinese writing was done with pictorial images, much as the Egyptian hieroglyphics, although the Chinese symbols showed more suggestion or imagination. These early pictorial symbols are still in use today. Chinese writing has changed little in nearly 2,000 years.

Chinese was the official script of Korea until the nineteenth century, even though a Korean alphabet was developed in 1447. Thus, traditional Korean calligraphy was done with Chinese characters.

Gradually Korea eliminated the Chinese characters and introduced a style of its own. Following World War II, however, calligraphy was treated as only a minor art up until the 1960s when the Korean government eliminated Chinese characters from the Korean language and began promoting the use of calligraphy in the Korean alphabet (Fig. 2-15).

In Japan, the art of calligraphy is as highly esteemed as it is in China. Japanese calligraphy began using Chinese characters at least as early as the end of the fourth century A.D. A great deal of Chinese calligraphy was imported to Japan through Chinese Buddhist monks who migrated there. This improved system of Chinese Buddhist calligraphy is called *kanji*.

Japan eventually devised its own form of calligraphy, called *hira-gana*. The elegant, graceful hand was often used for poetry. Both kanji and hira-gana are used in Japanese calligraphy today.

A SHORT HISTORY OF NUMERALS

Our numbering system has an entirely dif-

Fig. 2-14. An Italic headline.

Fig. 2-15. Korean calligraphy.

ferent basis than our alphabet. While our letters come from a Roman heritage, our numbers come from the Hindu culture.

The Hindu system of numbering was in use in India as early as the third century B.C. By about 700 A.D. the Arab world had adopted the Hindu numbers and rapidly became the dominant mathematical center of the world. From it the system we use still carries the name of Arabic Numerals.

The most important part of the Arabic Numeral system is the use of zero as a positional symbol, making it possible to differentiate between numbers such as 11 and 101 without the use of extra symbols.

While the Arabic Numeral system has come down through history to us intact, the form for writing the symbols has changed through the years. The basic style of numbers we use today was designed by Claude Garamont around the year 1545.

EARLY WRITING TOOLS

Writing has been done with a great variety of tools. Knives have been used to cut notches into sticks and to carve letters in other substances. Paint has been applied to many surfaces with brushes and quills. The Sumerians used pointed instruments on clay and a wedge-shaped reed on clay tablets. Reed pens, as well as brushes, were used by the Egyptians.

A principal early Greek writing tool was the stylus. It was used to incise wax tablets or the prepared surface of a skin, such as leather or vellum. Pens were used to write on papyrus. Also written on were lead, wood, pieces of pottery, and even cloth. The Greeks also probably conceived the idea of using a hard reed, split at the end and cut into a nib, as a pen.

Prior to about 300 A.D., ink was usually made of a carbon, such as lampblack, mixed with gum and water. This ink retains its rich black color even today. Because of the increasing popularity of vellum as a writing surface, iron inks became more widely used.

Papyrus and leather crafted for use as a writing material were normally sold in rolls made up of either 20 or 50 sheets glued together. With the beginning of the Christian Era came the custom of folding the sheets of papyrus or leather down the middle and stitching it into a binding case to form a book. The early Christians chose the book, or codex, form in which to circulate the Christian Gospels. By the fourth century A.D. it had become the dominant form.

A HISTORY OF PAPER

Credited with the invention of paper in the year 105 A.D. is Ts'ai Lun, a member of the Imperial Guard of the Later Han court of the Chinese emperor Ho Ti.

A mixture of mulberry bark, rags, and water was beaten into a pulp and left to dry in the sun on a mold of bamboo strips. The earliest known paper that still exists was made from rags in about 150 A.D.

For about 500 years paper was made only in China, but in 610 A.D. it was introduced into Japan and about 750 A.D., into Central Asia. Paper ap-

Fig. 2-16. Early freestyle majuscule alphabet.

Fig. 2-17. An informal alphabet.

peared in Egypt in about 800 A.D.

It was not until about 1150 that paper made its way to Europe, when the first paper-making mill was built in Spain. Over the next few centuries paper-making spread to most of the European countries, but it was not until the invention of movable type, about the middle of the fifteenth century, that book printing became practical, and paper was more in demand. The production of the Gutenberg Bible in 1456 helped stir an interest in paper and printing.

The first mill for making paper in England was established in 1495, and the first paper-making mill in the United States was constructed in 1690.

ABCDE FGHIK LMNOP QRSTU VWXYZ

Fig. 2-18. A Semi-block majuscule alphabet.

Paper was handmade one sheet at a time prior to the invention of the papermaking machine. Individual sheets were made by dipping a mold into a pulp mixture. The papermaking machine was an invention of Nicholas-Louis Robert of France in 1790. Robert's machine was improved by stationers and brothers Henry and Sealy Fourdrinier in England early in the nineteenth century.

The only inexpensive raw material used for paper until about 1840 was rags. For about 200 years many substitutes were tried in attempts to make paper more readily available. Around 1840 the process of grinding wood into pulp was discovered, and about ten years later the first of the chemical pulp processes emerged.

Currently the United States and Canada are the world's largest suppliers of paper, pulp, and paper products. Other significant paper producing countries are Finland, Japan, Sweden, and Russia.

CALLIGRAPHY TODAY

Calligraphy today is built upon a foundation that was begun when people first communicated silently. Tools and materials have changed dramatically through the years, leading to the sophisticated supplies available today.

The art of calligraphy is truly an accumulation of the history of writing, papers, alphabets, and tools. Because of the vast history of calligraphy, we not only have a variety of sophisticated materials and tools from which to choose, we have a number of calligraphic lettering styles from which to choose. Tools range from chisel-tip felt pins to professional calligraphers' pens to handmade pens. Papers that can be used include many inexpensive practice papers, machine-made special calligraphy papers, and expensive handmade papers.

Calligraphy styles to be studied of course include the five major historic styles Roman, Celtic,

Fig. 2-19. A Freehand alphabet.

Fig. 2-20. The Modified style.

Fig. 2-21. Modern ornate calligraphy.

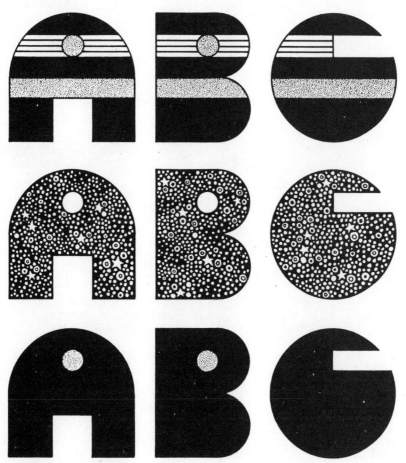

Fig. 2-22. Patterns can be used in calligraphy.

Gothic, Bookhand and Italic. Many variations of some styles exist. Many other calligraphy styles can also be learned (Figs. 2-16 through 2-22).

Throughout this book you will be introduced to both beginner and professional calligraphy equipment and supplies. Examples of many calligraphy styles will be presented.

Since you have been repeating the warm up exercises often and using your calligraphy pen regularly wherever you write, you should now be fairly comfortable with the pen and using it consistently at the correct 45-degree angle to the paper.

You are probably ready and anxious to move on and begin learning some real calligraphy. Chapter 3 will discuss the reasons for the focus on Italic writing; then it will introduce several basic-stroke exercises that will lead you into writing beautiful Italic letters.

3.
Basic
Calligraphy Strokes

Basic calligraphy can be both fun and easy. With just a few minutes' practice regularly, you can develop a whole new style of handwriting—one that will serve all your writing needs. Once you have learned the Italic modes of writing presented in this book, you may cease your studies and be content to perfect your new style of communicating. You may instead decide to continue studying and branch out to learn several other calligraphic forms, perhaps even becoming a professional calligrapher and setting up a commercial studio.

WHY BEGIN WITH ITALICS?

Italic handwriting is the style of calligraphy most often used. Italic letters were named for Renaissance Italy, which rapidly became a major cultural influence in the postmedieval world. A revival of Italic lettering occurred during the Arts and Crafts Movement of Europe in the late nineteenth century, and again during the current calligraphy revival, which began in the 1970s.

The recurring popularity of Italic writing is due to its beauty, ease of mastery, and adaptability. Variations of Italic writing make the style suitable for almost any written communication (Figs. 3-1 through 3-4).

This book will focus on two modes of Italic writing: Chancery Cursive and Straight, or Practical, Italics. The Chancery Cursive form is an elegant, flourished hand that is used for formal communications. It should not be used casually. Practical Italics, however, provide a writing style that is rapid, casual, and adapted to everyday use.

The letter slant, proportions, and oval shape are the same in Chancery Cursive and Practical Italics. The most significant difference is that Practical Italic letters do not employ *serifs*—extra, decorative lines that are placed on the open ends of basic letters—on the ascenders. For a really efficient lettering style, some writers eliminate serifs on descenders also. Italic writing is probably the only form of calligraphy that can fulfill both a formal and casual role without great variations from the basic form.

The Society for Italic Handwriting

Fig. 3-1. A popular form of Italic calligraphy.

Josephine's Patisserie
Aumsville

Fig. 3-2. An Italic show card.

Judy Ramsey

Caffé de Fina
Torte

Fig. 3-3. An Italic name tag.

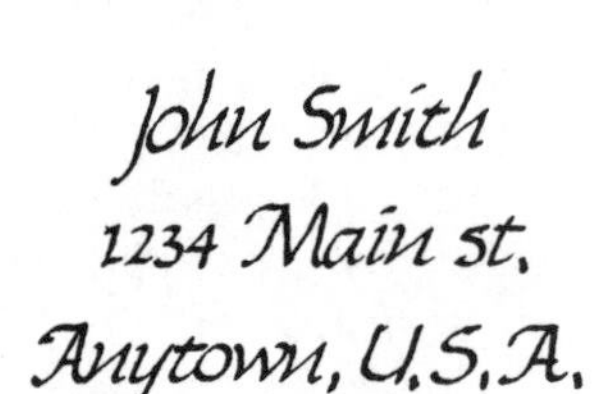

John Smith
1234 Main st.
Anytown, U.S.A.

Fig. 3-4. An Italic letterhead.

Italic calligraphy, based on the Classic Roman hand, is also flexible enough to allow personal interpretation to be incorporated into handwriting, without significantly altering that historic Roman beauty. It is an excellent choice for beginning study.

PREPARING TO MOVE ON

One of the most important considerations in learning any new skill or craft is to constantly review previous material and be sure that you are building your knowledge on a firm foundation. Let's make sure you are doing that with your calligraphy skills.

First, are you using a pen that will help advance your learning rapidly? The chisel-tip felt pen is the recommended instrument at this stage. The calligraphic fountain pen, which will be discussed in Chapter 5, will be recommended after you are thoroughly familiar with the formation of the Italic alphabet used for both Chancery Cursive and Practical Italics. The chisel-tip pen is better than a plain nylon-tip felt pen because it gives you the experience of working with a chiselled edge similar to that of the calligraphic fountain pen. With the chisel-tip pen you will be able to form the thick and thin portions of letters which make calligraphy distinctive.

By this time you should be getting familiar

with your pen, and it should be comfortable in your hand. When you practice your calligraphy exercises remember that your pen tip must be at a 45-degree angle to the paper in order for the ink to flow freely. Do a few rows of the second warm-up exercise to make sure you are holding the pen correctly to form the necessary angle.

You should be seated at your calligraphy desk with your body at approximately a 30-degree angle to the desk, sitting comfortably erect. If you are not relaxed, take a few minutes and do whatever it is that most helps you to relax.

Remember that in calligraphic writing, movement will come from your arm and shoulder. Your wrist and fingers should remain in a fixed position while your arm and shoulder move the pen across the page. Your effective working space is limited to about 5 inches. Move the paper when it is necessary to exceed this span, not your arm.

Have plenty of inexpensive practice paper handy. If you are using lined notebook paper or duplicator paper you can use it freely at small cost. Graph paper can be useful for checking for correct letter proportions. Use the paper that you like best, but for freehand lettering you should use a lined paper while learning to make your letters uniform. Use just one side of each sheet of paper so that it is easy to review your work and not confusing to make the letters.

Be sure your calligraphy table has the proper lighting in order to avoid eye-strain. Practice your calligraphy at a time and place when you can concentrate. Keep all your materials clean and wash your hands before you practice and often during practice if they become soiled.

Now do several rows of each of the six loosening-up exercises listed in Chapter 1. When you are done, go on to the next section, which will introduce the basic shapes which comprise Italic letters and basic stroke exercises. The basic stroke exercises will lead into the formation of Italic calligraphy letters.

THE BASIC ITALIC LETTERING STROKES

Italic letters are formed on two distinctly separate letter bodies. Once you are able to visualize this concept, you will understand how Italic letters are penned. The two separate shapes used in Italic letter bodies can be created by dividing a rectangle diagonally and adding either an upward or downward stroke. Go through the following steps to clarify this concept before you move on.

Step 1. See Fig. 3-5. Make the four straight illustrated pen strokes using a 45-degree pen angle. Notice that strokes 1 and 3 are longer than strokes 2 and 4, creating a rectangle, not a square.

Fig. 3-5. Step 1: use a 45-degree angle.

Step 2. See Fig. 3-6. Make the same rectangle with connected lines and at the Italic 5- or 10-degree slant to the right.

Fig. 3-6. Step 2: use a 10-degree slant.

Step 3. See Fig. 3-7. Divide the rectangle, going up. Then make each half of the rectangle separately.

Fig. 3-7. Step 3: make each half separately.

Step 4. See Fig. 3-8. Make each triangle again, adding a downstroke to the left-facing triangle and an upstroke to the right-facing triangle.

Fig. 3-8. Step 4: add a downstroke.

Step 5. See Fig. 3-9. Once again draw each triangle, but round off all corners. The two shapes you have created are the letter bodies upon which the Italic alphabet is built.

Fig. 3-9. Step 5: round off all corners.

Practice these five steps until they are familiar, and you can visualize how they will be built into Italic letters. Before you move on, your practice strokes should look very nearly like the examples.

The following exercises will make your hand familiar with the penning of other strokes that will be used in writing Italic calligraphy.

Exercise 7. This exercise will not only help with forming the letters n and m, but will reinforce the need to connect all down-strokes at the same point. Make the first downward stroke straight but slightly slanted (Fig. 3-10). Lift your pen and make the second stroke in an arch from just above the center of stroke 1 to the top of the line and down, parallel to stroke 1. Relax and don't rush. All of these exercises may first be traced and then drawn freehand.

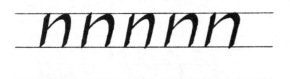

Fig. 3-10. Exercise 7: be sure to connect all downstrokes at the same point.

Exercise 8. This exercise provides good practice for making identical strokes (Fig. 3-11). The arched strokes should all be connected to the previous strokes at the same point.

Fig. 3-11. Exercise 8: make identical strokes.

Exercise 9. This exercise is just the opposite of Exercise 7. The inverted arch is made first, and the pen lifted for the final downward stroke (Fig. 3-12). All of these exercises should have the slight Italic slant to the right.

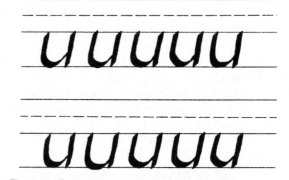

Fig. 3-12. Exercise 9: make the inverted arch first.

Exercise 10. Figure 3-13 shows a continuous line of the inverted arch. Strive for uniformity.

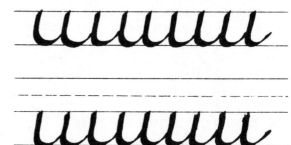

Fig. 3-13. Exercise 10: strive for uniformity.

Exercise 11. This exercise, shown in Fig. 3-14, alternates between the two shapes you have just learned. Trace several lines if you wish; then continue freehand until your strokes appear uniform, and the execution is comfortable.

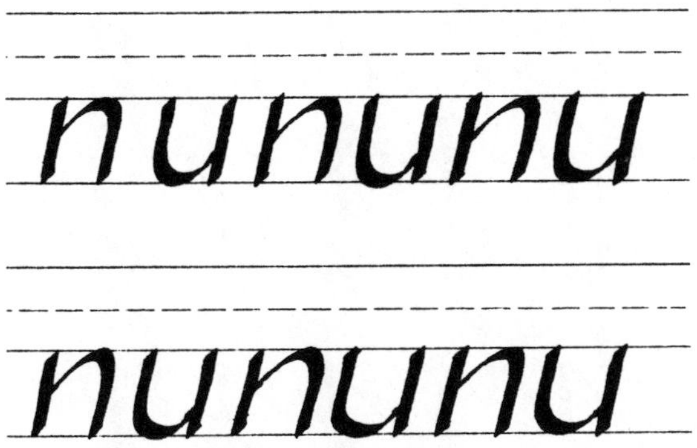

nununu

nununu

Fig. 3-14. Exercise 11: alternate the two shapes.

Take a break now and relax. Remember that our goal is fun and easy calligraphy. It won't be long until you can do any writing you wish in calligraphy. It is a rewarding learning process because you will be able to see improvement quickly. It is a skill that you can put to use immediately and without special effort. Right now you are getting extra practice by using your calligraphy pen whenever you write. The more familiar and comfortable you are with your pen, the easier it will be to learn letter strokes, and soon, Italic calligraphy letters. As soon as you learn the basic lettering techniques, you will be able to practice every time you write.

As suggested in Chapter 1, be sure to save some samples of your writing and practice sheets for review at various times through the learning process. Now let's return for some more basic stroke exercises.

Exercise 12. This exercise introduces the Italic o shape, which is actually oval and of course is at the slight right-hand slant (Fig. 3-15). Practicing it in conjunction with the straight down-stroke will help you to keep letter parts parallel as well as separate letters.

Exercise 13. This exercise will require the use of two ruled spaces. Begin the down-stroke at the top of the upper line, continue through the

OllOllOllOllO

OllOllOllOllO

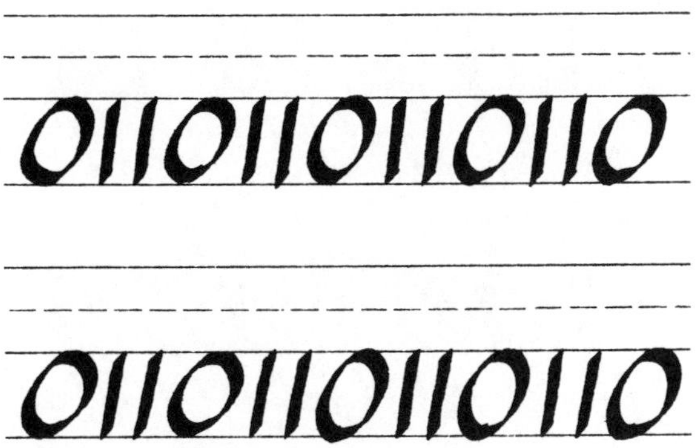

Fig. 3-15. Exercise 12: the Italic o.

center line, and end at the lower line (Fig. 3-16). The diagonal line stops at the center-ruled line, and the third stroke is downward parallel to the first stroke.

The next set of exercises will help you to learn basic letter shapes as well as help you later to join letters. They also are designed to develop rhythm and fluency.

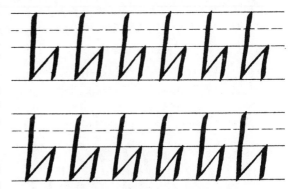

Fig. 3-16. Exercise 13: three strokes are made.

Exercise 14. This exercise also occupies two ruled spaces (Fig. 3-17). Stroke 1 begins slightly above the center line and ends at the top line. Stroke 2 goes all the way down to the bottom line where it forms a loop and moves into stroke 3, which ends at the same point where stroke 1 began, slightly above the center line.

Exercise 15. See Fig. 3-18. This exercise is simply a continuous line of the shape learned in Exercise 14.

Fig. 3-17. Exercise 14: end at the same point you began.

Fig. 3-18. Exercise 15: a continuous line.

Exercise 16. Figure 3-19 illustrates this exercise, which adds an upward stroke and loop into a downward stroke to the previously learned shape. It is an inversion of the same shape.

Fig. 3-19. Exercise 16: an inversion of the shape you just learned.

Exercise 17. In this exercise link a whole row of the upward and downward loops to further develop rhythm and fluency.

Fig. 3-20. Exercise 17: link a row of the loops.

Exercise 18. This exercise, as shown in Fig. 3-21, carries the linked loops a step further, moving directly from the upward loop to the downward loop. This shape covers three spaces on your prac-

Fig. 3-21. Exercise 18: covers three spaces.

tice paper if you are using ruled notebook paper. Beginning at the second line from the bottom, draw a diagonal line through the next line and up to the top line where the line curves and makes a long, slightly left-slanted line all the way to the bottom line. It then curves back upward, parallel to the beginning stroke and ends at the second line from the top.

Exercise 19. This exercise is simply a continuous line of the above exercise (Fig. 3-22) Your objective is to keep all parts of the shapes uniform and parallel.

Fig. 3-22. Exercise 19: keep all parts uniform and parallel.

Practice all of the exercises explained and illustrated in this chapter until you can rapidly and uniformly complete each. Go over these exercises, doing several rows of each at a time, until you are entirely comfortable drawing them and satisfied with the results. As you first begin to repeat the exercises you may, if you wish, begin by tracing each one several times. Keep working on them until you no longer need to trace, but can draw each set freely on your own.

When you are completely relaxed with these exercises and convinced that your attempts are nearly identical to the examples, you will be ready to move into learning Italic letters. Anytime through your studies that you feel awkward, return to these exercises and repeat each until you feel relaxed and comfortable again.

As you work into Chapter 4 and begin forming Italic letters you will see how the basic stroke exercises have helped to prepare you for actual calligraphic writing. The curves, shapes, slants and proportions are all used in Italic lettering. Your mastery of the letters will follow naturally and easily once you thoroughly study and practice the basic stroke exercises.

MORE ABOUT ITALIC WRITING

Italic calligraphy has many distinct characteristics, the most recognizable being its slight, 5- to 10-degree, right-hand slant. Italic letters are true to the Classic Roman models, but they add a great degree of uniformity to the alphabet.

Italic letters can be divided into four separate letter families. Two of those families are made up of the letters formed with the triangular letter bodies you studied earlier in this chapter. Let's call them the a-body family and the b-body family. Letters in the a-body family include a, c, d, e, g, q, u, and y. The b-body family consists of b, h, p, n, m, and r. Another family of special letters contains 1, f, t, i, v, w, k, and j. The last letter family includes o, s, x, and z, which connect points on the Italic rectangle.

Written with a 45-degree pen-to-paper angle, Italic minuscules should be approximately five pen widths high, and majuscules should be about seven pen widths high. A pen width means the width of the pen nib, or point. For practice purposes, the ruled lines on notebook paper are sufficient.

Several techniques exist for spacing between letters in Italic writing and for joining letters in Chancery Cursive and Practical Italics. These will be studied in depth in a later chapter. You will be encouraged to try many different approaches to joining letters. You will discover that some letters do not join gracefully with any other letter. Eventually you will choose your own methods of joining letters; this is another example of where individuality can be inserted into your calligraphy. Italic writing is characterized by a minimum of pen lifts, using both pushing and pulling strokes. Joins can be with diagonal or horizontal lines, and they sometimes call for the addition of a curve.

Italic writing appears with or without serifs. You will learn the Practical Italics, without serifs, and the Chancery Cursive, with serifs.

Your study of Italic calligraphy can lead to anything from improved handwriting to a career as a professional calligrapher.

HOW CALLIGRAPHY COMMUNICATES

Calligraphic writing communicates more than just the written word. The thought message of course is the most important, but calligraphy provides a special way of conveying the idea and offers ways of intensifying the effect of the message.

Beautiful writing also communicates visually. A feeling of warmth or of formality can be imparted by your choice of style. Elegance is often suggested by calligraphic writing. A message communicated through a beautiful medium is memorable. Historically some calligraphic forms relied on drawings or paintings incorporated into the manuscript to help clarify the meaning of the script. This method was especially prevalent and important when literacy was confined to a small portion of the population.

Calligraphy communicates through materials. The choice of mundane or special inks (Fig. 3-23) and papers (Fig. 3-24) can have an impact on the message the calligraphy is intended to impart. Calligraphy can be used on poster paper to announce a special event, or elegant, handmade paper can be used to issue invitations to an event. The calligrapher's choice of materials makes a statement about the content of the message.

By careful choice of calligraphy style, attention to ornateness or casualness, selection of appropriate inks and papers, and choice of a suitable message, a calligrapher can create a piece of handiwork that communicates visually and intellectually through expert craftsmanship.

Fig. 3-23. There are numerous inks available to the calligrapher.

42

Fig. 3-24. A variety of calligraphy papers.

THE IMPORTANCE OF CONCENTRATION AND PRACTICE

Concentration is a key factor in the learning and execution of calligraphy. Expert calligraphers teach serious students special breathing techniques. Our focus is on easy calligraphy, however; so it would not be appropriate to attempt to teach on an expert level. For those who decide to become serious calligraphy students after completing this book, there will be suggestions later in the text about how and where to continue further studies.

Concentration is necessary to receive the most benefit from any study, and this is true of *easy* calligraphy. It is vital to clear your mind of day-to-day problems, and give all your attention to your studies and practice.

By this time you probably have established a regular practice schedule. If you have not, set one up now so that you maintain a flow and gain momentum in your studies. With regular practice you will find that your skills grow more rapidly. Your practice time need not be lengthy; 20 minutes is sufficient as long as it is regular—if not every day at least three times a week.

Your regular study of calligraphy will not only serve to improve your penmanship and learn new styles of writing, it will develop your sense of self-discipline and also foster creativity. The craft of calligraphy is open to everyone; you can easily attain the necessary skill through regular, fun-to-do practice.

THE CALLIGRAPHIC FOUNTAIN PEN

The choice of when to advance to a calligraphic fountain pen is entirely yours. You are the best judge of your own progress. Remember to work at your own pace and continue with the chisel-tip felt pen until you feel a real urge to move on. You can also use your chisel-tip pen through all your calligraphy studies.

It is recommended that you wait to use the calligraphic pen until you have become familiar with minuscule and majuscule Italic letters. Waiting is recommended because it is easiest to learn when only faced with one change at a time.

You may already feel the need to use a calligraphic fountain pen, however, that's fine too. In case you are ready, I will discuss the calligraphic fountain pen now. The use of a special calligraphic pen, which must be dipped in ink, is not yet recommended. At this point it is of more value to you as a student to concentrate on penmanship—forming your calligraphy letters correctly and uniformly. Later in the book true calligraphy pens will be discussed in case you wish to carry your studies further.

The calligraphy fountain pen differs from a regular fountain pen in two main ways: the nib and the ink flow. Calligraphic fountain pen nibs come in a variety of widths making possible many changes in writing character. The nib or point of the pen is not square. It will draw the finest line when moved upward from left to right at the 45-degree angle, and the widest line when moved down from left to right at the same angle. By changing the angle of pen to paper the width of the line drawn can be varied.

Several satisfactory calligraphy fountain pens are available at variety, stationery, or art supply stores. Among them are the Platignum, Osmiroid, and Sheaffer calligraphy fountain pens. Slightly more expensive, and of a little better quality, is the Pelikan calligraphy fountain pen. With care any of these pens will last for many years. Some are cartridge-type pens, and some have ink reservoirs which must be filled with a bottle of ink.

Your pen is made up of four parts. They are the nib unit, the ink reservoir (or cartridge), the barrel, and the cap (Fig. 3-25). Figures 3-26 and 3-27 show how to assemble a cartridge pen.

To fill a reservoir-type pen, screw the nib into the reservoir and hold it so the ink just covers the nib. Squeeze the metal band around the reservoir four or five times and it should be filled. Wipe off excess ink, and you should be ready to write. If your pen has a lever on the side of the barrel, you must screw the nib and reservoir into the barrel before filling. Fill as a regular fountain pen, by holding the nib in the ink and lifting the lever four or five times. Wipe off the extra ink.

Try your pen. Remember that the entire edge of the nib must be on the paper for ink to flow. If the ink will not flow even with the entire nib edge on the paper, drop it *lightly* on its tip to force the ink to begin to flow. Holding your pen at a 45-degree angle, make a series of different strokes. Watch how your pen works. Take your time and get to know your calligraphy fountain pen well. Your pen is your most important calligraphy tool. The better you know it, the better it will be able to serve your needs.

If the pen you have chosen is a reservoir type, be sure you always use a special calligraphy ink. India ink can clog your pen and is therefore not suitable for the fountain pen. Plain fountain pen ink is thin and does not create crisp letters. Good choices of ink for student calligraphers include Higgins Eternal Ink and Pelikan 4001 ink.

Some pen manufacturers suggest that you clean your pen thoroughly every two weeks. To clean it, empty the pen, separate all the parts, rinse thoroughly under running water, and dry thoroughly.

Using a medium nib (Fig. 3-28), go back through the loosening-up and basic stroke exercises and get used to your new pen. The medium nib

Fig. 3-25. A calligraphic fountain pen.

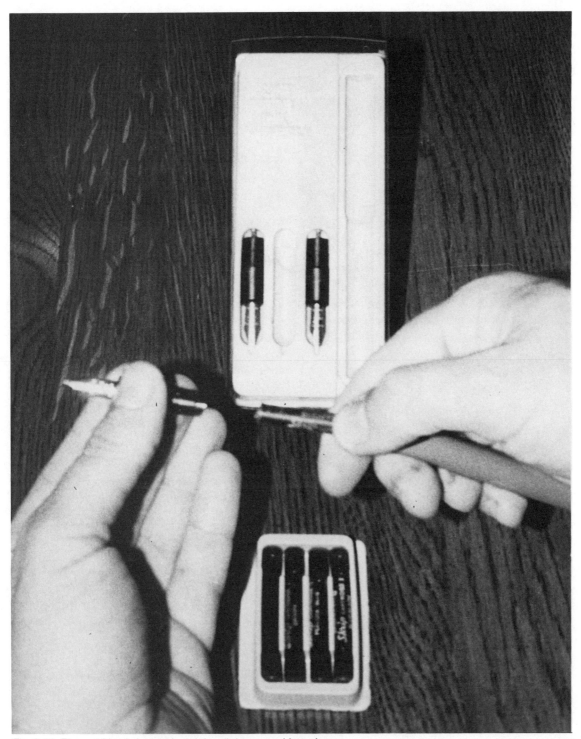

Fig. 3-26. The cartridge is inserted, and the nib is screwed into place.

Fig. 3-27. The cartridge fountain pen is assembled.

Fig. 3-28. This is the width of a medium nib.

will serve your needs through the rest of this book.

Remember that the choice of when to advance to a calligraphy fountain pen is completely personal.

If you feel ready, by all means change now. If you wish, change once you are familiar with the Italic letter formations, or, continue with your chisel-tip pen throughout your studies with this book. Calligraphy is an individual craft which you can personalize by your choices of tools, materials, and styles of writing. Take advantage of this characteristic. Follow your own instincts.

WHAT COMES NEXT

You are probably anxious to get started actually writing calligraphy letters. In fact you may have looked ahead and made a few attempts to copy the Italic letters. Your patience will soon be rewarded.

You are now comfortable with the strokes that will make up Italic letters. Your hand has become used to letting your shoulder and arm do most of the work of writing. You recognize Italic lettering and know the theory behind the formation of the letters.

You are ready to begin practicing Italic letters. Chapter 4 will discuss Italic minuscules. Letters will be introduced in families, and practice exercises will be outlined. You will learn about the anatomy of a letter; common lettering mistakes and their solutions. You will practice word lists and sentences to sharpen your skills.

By the end of Chapter 4 you will be able to write a complete Italic minuscule alphabet. Chapter 5 will add majuscules, and then you will be able to execute your first calligraphy project.

Keep up your faithful practice, and you will be a calligrapher in a very short time.

4.

Forming
Calligraphic Letters

Your first calligraphic alphabet will be minuscule, or lower case, Practical Italics. You will learn and practice letters in the letter families identified in Chapter 3. The letters are grouped by shape rather than alphabetically. You will begin with the a-body family.

To learn most effectively, use the following method with each new lesson:

- Read the instructions,
- Study the illustrations,
- Trace the letters,
- Draw the letters freely until they look nearly like the examples.

On your practice paper, the line that the body of each letter rests on is called the *base line*. The line above it, which comes at the top of letters such as a, c, m, and o, is called the *waist line*. *Ascenders* are letters such as l and k, that extend above the waist line. *Descenders,* such as j, and p, are letters that continue below the base line.

THE a-BODY FAMILY

Many calligraphers consider the minuscule "a"

to be the most difficult Italic letter to master. Once you understand and can form the letter a correctly, however, you will have the basis for the entire a-family of letters. Remember that the a-body letters are based on the left-facing triangle that is formed by diagonally bisecting a slightly right-slanting, standing rectangle. (See Chapter 3.)

Exercise 20. (Fig. 4-1) shows you the correct formation of the letter a. It is made with one stroke beginning at the waist line, with your pen touching the paper at a 45-degree angle. Your pen will travel to the left along the waist line, then descend to the base line at a slight right-hand slant. The pen then angles back upward to the waist line to the beginning of the letter, leaving an almost pointed corner at the base line. The stroke then comes back down to the base line on the same slight slant. Practice this letter until you are quite confident of its execution. It is your first true calligraphy letter, and it also forms the basis for several other Italic letters.

When you practice individual letters, or letter families, keep the letters close together. This will help you to get the feeling of true spacing for when

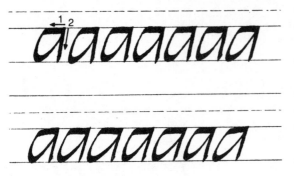

Fig. 4-1. Exercise 20: the correct formation of an a.

Fig. 4-3. Exercise 22: your first ascender.

you begin writing in calligraphy. Spacing between letters is extremely important to the look of calligraphy.

Exercise 21. This exercise simply adds a descender to the letter a to turn it into either the letter q or the letter g (Fig. 4-2). The q is formed by a descender that slants to the right and ends at the line below the base line on your practice sheet. The g is formed with a descender that slants to the right and ends in a curve to the left.

Fig. 4-2. Exercise 21: add a descender.

Exercise 22. In this exercise, you will form your first ascender, the letter d (Fig. 4-3). It is created by two strokes. The first stroke is identical to the beginning of the a, stopping on the up-swing after making the nearly pointed corner at the base line. Lift your pen and make an ascender from the top line, through the waist line, and on down to the base line. The ascender should touch the two ends of the first stroke.

Exercise 23. (Fig. 4-4) shows you the letter c, which is formed like the beginning of the a. Place your pen at the waist line, stroke left and curve down to the base line, where you form the almost pointed curve that ends the c. Once your c is drawn correctly the e will follow naturally.

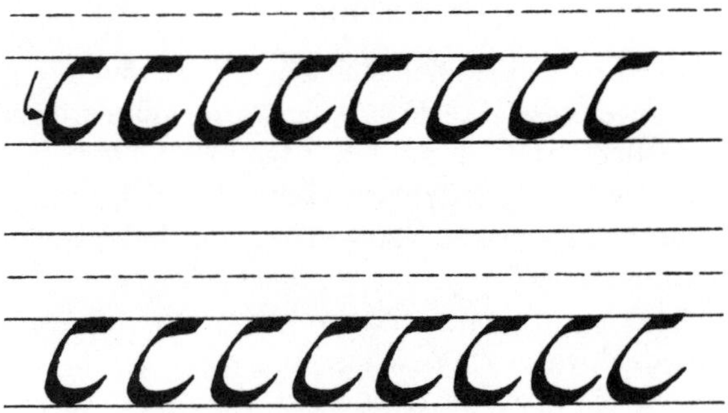

Fig. 4-4. Exercise 23: the letter c.

Exercise 24. This exercise adds another stroke to the c to turn it into the letter e (Fig. 4-5). Beginning a little more than halfway between the base and waist lines, stroke diagonally up to the waist line, then continue as you did for the c.

Move slowly through all these letter exercises. The more practice you put into learning the formation of the letters, the stronger will be your calligraphy background. You will very soon be able to use your new style of handwriting any time you like.

Fig. 4-5. Exercise 24: turn a c into an e.

Exercise 25. This exercise uses one of the basic calligraphy strokes you learned earlier to create the letters u and y Fig. 4-6). The u begins at the waist line, descends at a slant to the base line, curves back up to the waist line, and descends again to the base line. To form the y, make a u and continue the last downstroke as a descender that ends in a left curve at the line below the base line.

Fig. 4-6. Exercise 25: create a u and a y.

Now you have learned your first group of Practical Italic letters, the a-body family. You can use these letters to begin practicing with complete words. Here are some possibilities: dad, age, quad, day, gauge, guy, deuce, cage, gay, and quay. Make

up your own list. Your list of practice words will become endless as you add letters while moving on through your studies.

THE b-BODY LETTERS

When you feel completely at ease with the a-body family of letters, continue with the following exercises. They introduce the b-body family of letters, consisting of b, h, p, n, m, and r.

Repetitious practice makes for a good calligrapher. Keep that in mind when you get tired of one letter and want to move quickly on to another. We have moved slowly through our study of calligraphy for good reason. The better your basic calligraphy strokes and letters, the better will be your calligraphy projects in the future. Take your time now and learn the basics thoroughly, and you will be pleased with the results. Your handwriting will be admired; you will be able to create beautiful gifts and home decorations, and you will be able to easily move into advanced calligraphy studies, if you take the time now to get to know your new craft intimately.

Exercise 26. Figure 4-7 teaches the minuscule b. With your pen at the top line, draw a slightly right-slanted line down through the waist line, ending at the base line. Curve over to the waist line; then curve back down to the base line, and draw a flat stroke along the base line to meet the initial downstroke. The curve at the base line should be almost pointed.

Fig. 4-7. Exercise 26: the miniscule b.

Exercise 27. This exercise modifies the b to make a Practical Italics h, also made with two strokes (Fig. 4-8). Beginning at the line above the waist line, draw a slightly right-slanted stroke all the way to the base line. Lift your pen and start the second stroke a little more than halfway between the base and waist lines, touching the first stroke. Curve up to the waist line and back down, parallel to the first stroke, to the base line.

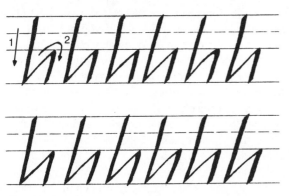

Fig. 4-8. Exercise 27: make an h.

Exercise 28. Figure 4-9 shows you that the letter p contains a body of the same shape as the b. To complete a letter p, draw a 5- or 10-degree slanted line from the waist line to the line below the base line and curve left. Lift your pen and, beginning near the top of the first line, make the curved part of the body just as you made the body of the b.

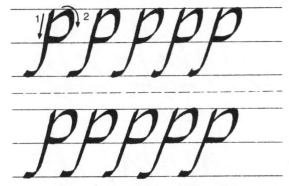

Fig. 4-9. Exercise 28: the letter p.

Exercise 29. This exercise shows you how to create the letter n, using a familiar basic calligraphy stroke (Fig. 4-10). Touch the paper with your pen at the waist line and make a slanted line just to the base line. Lift your pen and start the second stroke near the bottom of the first. Curve up to the waist line and come down to the base line parallel to the first stroke. The n is like an h without the ascender.

Fig. 4-10. Exercise 29: create an n.

Exercise 30. This exercise takes the n one step further to make an m (Fig. 4-11). Just add a third stroke identical to the second stroke of the n, taking care that both strokes begin at the same level.

Fig. 4-11. Exercise 30: now make an m.

Exercise 31. Figure 4-12 introduces the last member of the b-body family, the r. The r requires two strokes and begins just like the letter n, with a straight, but slightly slanted, stroke from the waist line to the base line. Lift the pen and make a second

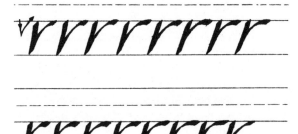

Fig. 4-13. Exercise 32: the letter l.

Fig. 4-12. Exercise 31: the last member of the b family.

short stroke from near the top of the first to the waist line, with just a slight curve back down toward the base line.

Now you have completed the exercises covering all of the letters in the b-body family. You have learned to form more than half of the letters of the alphabet. With the 14 letters you know, you can make up a list of many practice words to add variety to your studies.

Take a few minutes now and review your progress in your calligraphy studies. Look at your first attempts at reproducing the loosening-up exercises from Chapter 1. Compare them with the loosening-up exercises you executed yesterday. By now you should be consistently holding your calligraphy pen at the right angle and using your shoulder and arm to move the pen. These things, as well as your growing confidence and skill, will be evident in your writing practice. Your recent loosening-up exercises should be more consistent and more surely drawn than your earlier attempts, and the learning process has been easy.

SPECIAL LETTERS

The family of special letters consists of those letters that do not fit into one or the other categories. They include the l, f, t, i, v, w, k, and j.

Exercise 32. Figure 4-13 introduces the one-stroke letter l. To make an l, simply make a down-stroke from the line above the waist line, down through the waist line, ending at the base line. It is identical to the first stroke in the letter b.

Exercise 33. Figure 4-14 illustrates the letter f. Beginning at the midpoint between the waist line and the next higher line, curve slightly to the left into a downstroke that ends one line below the base line with another curve to the left. Cross the first stroke at the waist line.

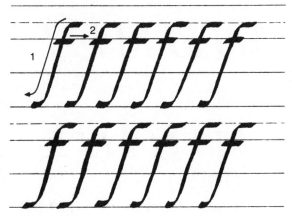

Fig. 4-14. Exercise 33: make an f.

Exercise 34. Figure 4-15 shows how to create the letter t, which is made with two quick

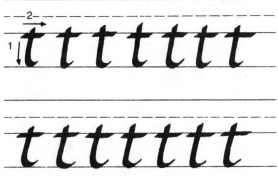

Fig. 4-15. Exercise 34: two quick strokes make a t.

strokes. Stroke one begins just above the waist line and ends with a small hook at the base line. The cross to the t is at the waist line.

Exercise 35. This exercise shows the letter i (Fig. 4-16). Beginning with a small hook to the left at the waist line, the pen then strokes down at a slight slant to the base line, ending with a small hook to the right. The i is dotted with just a pen touch above it.

Practice each letter until you are comfortable with it. This chapter will probably take the most study time. Be patient with yourself, proceed slowly, practice regularly, and enjoy learning calligraphy easily.

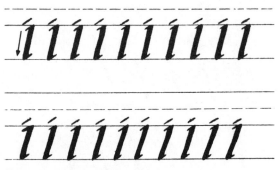

Fig. 4-16. Exercise 35: the letter i.

Exercise 36. This exercise shows you how to make the letter v (Fig. 4-17). A small hook to the left starts the letter at the waist line. Then stroke at a slant to the base line and curve back up to the waist line, ending with a hook to the left. There

Fig. 4-17. Exercise 36: a small hook starts a v.

should be a point where the bottom of the v touches the base line.

Exercise 37. This exercise adds to the v to make a w (Fig. 4-18). The first half of the w is penned precisely as the v. When the second stroke of the v is completed, curve back down to the base line again, and once more back up to the waist line ending with a hook to the left. There is the w.

Fig. 4-18. Exercise 37: now make a w.

Exercise 38. Figure 4-19 introduces the letter k. Touch your pen to the paper at the line above the waist line. Stroke all the way down to the base line. Lift your pen and touch down again at the first line just below the waist line. Make a small curve up to the waist line and back to the first stroke just below where the second stroke originated. Then curve on down to the base line and end with a small hook to the right.

Fig. 4-19. Exercise 38: the k ends with a hook.

Exercise 39. This exercise brings the last letter of this family, the j (Fig. 4-20). The j begins with a hook that touches the bottom of the waist

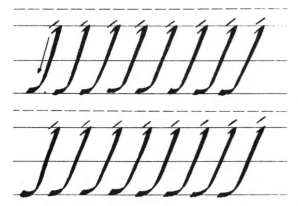

Fig. 4-20. Exercise 39: the letter j.

line. Next, stroke down to the line below the base line and end with a left curve. Touch the pen above the top of the letter to dot the j.

Now you have learned the family of special letters. Practice them, and the a-body and b-body letters, for as long as you need. Practicing the letters is the whole key to learning calligraphy.

You have only four more letters to learn.

RECTANGLE-CONNECTING LETTERS

The last Practical Italics letter family consists of the letters that connect the points on the Italic rectangle. They are the o, s, x, and z.

Exercise 40. Figure 4-21 shows you how to draw the important letter o. The o is actually made in an oval shape. The letter begins at the waist line, curves down to the base line and back up to the waist line. Notice in the illustration that the bottom of the o is almost pointed where it begins its ascent

Fig. 4-21. Exercise 40: an oval o.

back up to the waist line. Remember to maintain the Italic right-hand slant.

Exercise 41. Figure 4-22 illustrates the letter s. Beginning at the waist line, stroke left, then reverse and make a diagonal stroke to the right all the way to the base line, then again stroke left. This is all done without lifting the pen from the paper. Note that the places where you change directions should be almost pointed, rather than curved.

Fig. 4-22. Exercise 41: the letter s.

Exercise 42. Figure 4-23 shows you the letter x. Two strokes are necessary. The first begins with a slight hook at the waist line, then travels diagonally to the right down to the base line, ending with a slight hook. The second stroke also begins at the waist line, just to the right of the beginning of the first stroke. It extends diagonally to the left, crossing the middle of the first stroke, and ends on the base line with no hooks.

Fig. 4-23. Exercise 42: two strokes make an x.

Exercise 43. This exercise brings you the last letter of the alphabet, z (Fig. 4-24). The z is

Fig. 4-24. Exercise 43: the last letter of the alphabet.

made without lifting the pen from the paper. Beginning at the waist line with a hook, make a short stroke to the right, then move diagonally to the left to the base line, and finally draw a short stroke to the right ending with a hook.

You have now learned the entire minuscule Practical Italics alphabet. Your opportunities for practice are now unlimited. Use calligraphy when you write notes, make a grocery list, write checks, and any other time you write informally. Once you have learned the minuscule forms of Practical Italics you will be ready to use your calligraphy any time. Majuscules will be presented later in this chapter.

ANATOMY OF A LETTER

Each letter of the alphabet is made up of as many as six separate parts. They are the body, ascender, counter, serif, and descender. Let's take a look at each part.

The *body* of the minuscule letter is that portion which appears between the waist and base lines.

An *ascender,* as we have seen, is the part of the letter that rises above the body, extending over the waist line.

In contrast, the *descender* is the part of a letter that extends below the base line, below the body of the letter.

A *counter* is the open space within a letter. It can be either enclosed or open. We will be looking at counters and letter spacing soon. Both are vital to the apperance of calligraphy.

Serifs are the extra, decorative lines that are placed on the open ends of basic letters. These will become important when you begin to learn to form Chancery Cursive letters.

SPACING AND JOINING LETTERS

As an aid in learning proper spacing and proportions within and between letters, counters can actually be drawn at these places. A counter for Practical Italics should be drawn as an oblong ⅓ as high as the space between the waist and base lines. Counters should be drawn as closely as possible to the vertical lines of a letter. Use a different color ink for the counters to make it easier to visualize the concept of spacing. Try the following exercise.

Exercise 44. This exercise will check your spacing within letters. Draw the series of connected shapes shown in Fig. 4-25 with your regular calligraphy pen. With another color ink, draw counters within each space. If oblongs one third as high as the space between the waist and base lines cannot be drawn between the vertical strokes, practice the exercise until they can fit. Proper proportions and spacing are a part of the beauty of calligraphy.

The same counter system is used to determine proper spacing between letters, whether they stand alone or are joined.

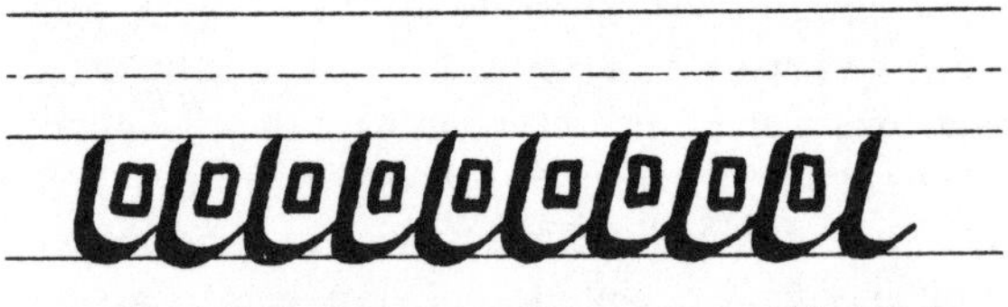

Fig. 4-25. Exercise 44: check your spacing within letters.

Exercise 45. Figure 4-26 illustrates the counter system for spacing between letters. One counter should fit between two letters. Draw a series of letters and insert counters between each in a different color ink. The counters should be placed beside the widest part of each letter. This counter system will also be used for spacing when joining letters.

Spacing between words is just as easily achieved. To learn proper spacing between words, simply insert a minuscule Practical Italics o between the words.

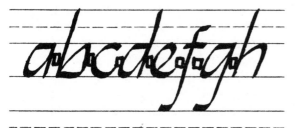

Fig. 4-26. Exercise 45: how to space between letters.

Exercise 46. This exercise is for practice in spacing between words. Write a number of words with your regular pen. With another color ink, insert an o between each word (Fig. 4-27).

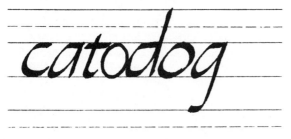

Fig. 4-27. Exercise 46: space between words.

If you spend a little time now studying and practicing proper spacing within and between letters and between words, you will quickly and easily learn to space correctly when writing freehand. Once you are confident of the formation and spacing of Practical Italics letters, you will be ready to learn to join letters so you can use this style of writing every day.

Practical Italics letters are designed for easy joining and efficient, speedy writing. Even so, you will find that some letters do not join gracefully, such as the b. While you are learning the Practical Italics style as an everyday hand, do not try for so much speed that you sacrifice the beauty that is the essence of calligraphy. Join letters when feasible, but take the time to create individual letters when necessary for a better appearance.

Many ways of joining can be used. Try them all and decide which is the best for you. Remember to keep joining lines light and thin by lifting your pen slightly when joining letters.

For the purposes of joining, letters will be divided into three groups, according to ways they can be joined. The first group consists of letters that end on an upstroke: a, c, d, h, i, k, l, m, n, and u. The second group includes letters that begin on an upstroke: i, j, m, n, p, r, t, u, v, w, x, and y. The third group consists of letters that can be joined by having them touch on the way down: a, c, d, e, g, and q. You will notice that a few letters appear in more than one group.

Three major ways of joining letters work best with Practical Italics letters. They are the diagonal join, the horizontal join, and the touch join. Experiment with all three and decide which way you like best. You may decide to use only one style of joining, or you can easily use whichever style works best for each letter or combination of letters.

Exercise 47. Figure 4-28 illustrates diagonal joins; they are used when letters from group one are followed by letters from group two. To join,

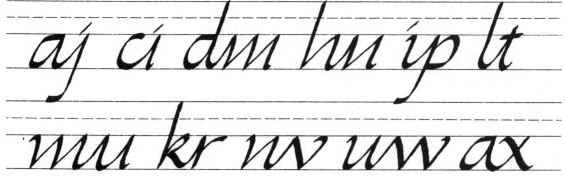

Fig. 4-28. Exercise 47: diagonal joins.

simply continue the upstroke of the first letter until it becomes the downstroke of the following letter

Exercise 48. This exercise demonstrates the use of the horizontal join, which necessitates the use of a heavier joining line (Fig. 4-29). The horizontal join is mainly used with the letters t and f, and is a continuation of the cross of the t or f to a letter that connects naturally. The horizontal join is also sometimes used with the letter o to connect it to the next letter, if it can be done gracefully.

Fig. 4-29. Exercise 48: the horizontal join.

Exercise 49. The touch join is used when two letters cannot be joined horizontally or vertically, but their strokes can touch, appearing as a join. Figure 4-30 gives some examples for you to try.

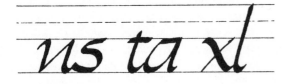

Fig. 4-30. Exercise 49: the touch join.

A few letters either do not join well with other letters with any method, or they require a special joining method. The letters b and s are generally not joined, although the s can sometimes appear joined when it follows a letter that ends on an upstroke.

The letters l, h, and k are not usually joined to the letters before them, but they can be joined to letters that follow, because they end on an upstroke. The letters g, y, j, and q are not joined unless the tails are made into loops.

Exercise 50. Figure 4-31 presents two methods of joining the letter e. It joins like the c to letters preceding it, but either of the two ways illustrated can be used to join it to letters that follow. Experiment with each until you choose one; then use it consistently.

Fig. 4-31. Exercise 50: two ways to join the e.

Exercise 51. The letter r is another individual choice. Figure 4-32 shows different ways of joining the r to letters that come before and after it. Try them all and decide which you wish to use.

Fig. 4-32. Exercise 51: how to join the r.

Exercise 52. Finally, the letters v, w, x, and z join easily to many letters that come before them, but look best if not joined to a following letter (Fig. 4-33).

Fig. 4-33. Exercise 52: joining v, w, and x.

Take the time to experiment extensively with each style of joining letters. Try them until you find the combinations that best suit your own personal style of Practical Italics calligraphic handwriting. Establishing a consistent style for joining letters will help to build the most efficient and attractive everyday handwriting possible.

To complete your first entire alphabet, let's examine Practical Italics majuscules.

PRACTICAL ITALIC MAJUSCULES

Practical Italic majuscules, or capitals, will be easy to learn. You already know the basics from studying the minuscules, or lower case letters, and from your familiarity with Roman Capitals.

Turn your imagination and creativity loose as you design your own individual set of capital letters to use with your everyday style of writing. A set of majuscules is presented here as an example, but feel free to make changes. Do remember, however, that majuscules should be approximately ¾ the height of a minuscule l, or seven pen widths high. If you keep the tops of your majuscules about halfway between the waist line and the top line, you will not need to measure.

Exercise 53. Practical Italic majuscules for your everyday writing should be kept simple. They look best when they are wide and angular. Practice the capitals illustrated in Fig. 4-34 several times; then break away from them and make your own variations. Eventually you will determine a set of capitals that reflect your own individuality. Again, use your creativity and take plenty of time to find your own style. Once you have found that personal style, however, be consistent.

You now have a complete alphabet, including capitals, with which to work and practice. Use your calligraphy. Write to friends, begin a personal journal, or copy a favorite quotation or poem. Any writing that you do will help to strengthen your calligraphy skills.

SOME COMMON MISTAKES AND THEIR SOLUTIONS

Now that you have been practicing your calligraphy letters for several days, let's look at some common mistakes that beginners make. If you are making any of the following mistakes, make a concentrated effort to change your habits now. It will be much easier now than later, and the results of your calligraphy efforts will be more satisfactory if your letters are correctly and proportionately drawn.

Early common mistakes usually involve an-

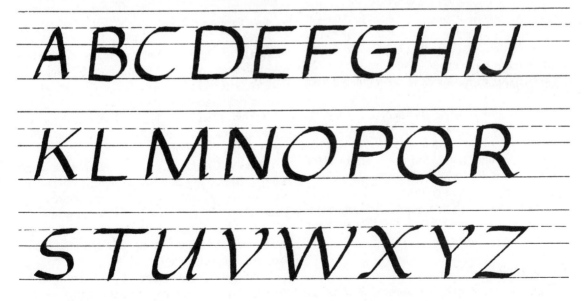

Fig. 4-34. Exercise 53: make majuscules angular.

gles, either too rounded or too pointed; letters, too narrow or too wide; curves, either too straight or too curved, or the wrong letter slant (Fig. 4-35).

Check letters such as the i, l, and t for hook ends that are too round or too pointed. The flip up at the base line is made by lifting your pen quickly at the end of the letter. Match this carefully because the small hook at the end of the letter occurs frequently in Italics. Other angles that can become too rounded or too pointed are at the top of the body of letters such as the h, m, n, b, and k.

Many letters can also appear too narrow or too wide (Fig. 4-36). This is most evident in letters such as the r, n, m, and w. If the letters are too narrow, the writing looks crowded, and if the letters are too wide, the writing begins to look scrawled. If your letters look either too narrow or too wide, return to the section on counters and repeat the exercises designed to help you learn the proper proportioning of letters.

Curves on letters such as j, y, p, and q can become too curved or end without enough curve (Fig. 4-37). A slight curving back up from the base line is all that is required.

The correct letter slant is vital to Italic writing; it is one of the style's most distinctive characteristics. A slight 5- or 10-degree slant to the right is correct. Letters that are too slanted look out of kilter, and letters that are straight up and down do not fit with the Italic image.

If you are having any of these problems with your writing, take the time to do some extra practicing before you move on to Chapter 5. Concentrate on any letters that are giving you trouble. Do a few extra rows of each problem letter. Review the exercises explaining how to form each letter and try to make your letters look as nearly like the illustrations as possible. If you continue to have trouble with a particular letter, find a similarly formed letter and practice it. Then return to the difficult letter and it may come easier.

LOOK AT YOUR PROGRESS

You now have a solid basic knowledge of calligraphy, specifically Practical Italics. You have

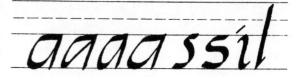

Fig. 4-35. Common mistakes.

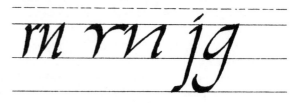

Fig. 4-36. Incorrect spacing.

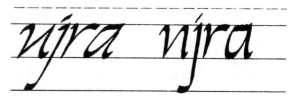

Fig. 4-37. Incorrect slanting.

learned a complete alphabet that can be used in all of your everyday writing. In Chapter 5, Chancery Cursive letters will be introduced. Once you have learned the Chancery Cursive mode, you will have two styles of writing. They can be used for any occasion: Practical Italics for informal, and Chancery Cursive for formal.

Also in Chapter 5 you will learn more about using calligraphy—how to paragraph, break up text, divide words, punctuate, and abbreviate. These are the things you will need to know in order to create your first calligraphy project. You will learn more about evaluating your calligraphy and how to correct mistakes.

You have learned one style of calligraphic writing. All you need now to perfect that hand is practice. With practice will come a feel for correct proportion, uniformity, and fluency. If you end your study of calligraphy right now, you have already learned a new type of writing that can be useful. If you choose to continue, however, you can quickly and easily build on that foundation and become a devoted calligrapher.

5.

Building
Your Skills

Your practice and study of calligraphy can go on for years. You will become more and more expert as you use your calligraphy. You can also go on to learn several alphabets: Gothic, Celtic, Bookhand, or less well-known hands such as Copperplate and French Roundhand.

Once you have mastered the Practical Italics and become adept at Chancery Cursive, which will be presented in this chapter, you will have learned the two most useful calligraphy styles. You will be able to use your skills to create informal or formal calligraphy projects.

THE CHANCERY CURSIVE STYLE

The design of the ornate Chancery Cursive mode of Italic handwriting is attributed to Ludovico degli Arrighi, early in the 16th century. Although the term *cursive* means any writing that is connected, and is usually meant for everyday use, Chancery Cursive is more flourished and not really suitable for everyday use. Many calligraphers consider Chancery Cursive to be the most beautiful

Italic style, and of course Italics in general is the most popular calligraphy style.

Chancery Cursive letters are oval, as are Practical Italic letters, and have long ascenders and descenders, which are bent. The slight right-hand slant is characteristic of all Italic lettering. Chancery Cursive letters should be approximately five pen widths high. Lined notebook paper is ruled at about the right width. The letters are written with the pen touching the paper at about a 45-degree angle.

Basically, Chancery Cursive letters are formed like Practical Italic letters. The bodies are identical. The difference lies in the ascenders and sometimes in the descenders. Practical Italics actually represent a simplified version of Chancery Cursive. Practical Italic letters are simple and unadorned. Chancery Cursive letters employ swashes on the ascenders which give the style its ornate appearance. A *swash* is an extra horizontal stroke on the right of an ascender or the left of a descender.

Exercise 54. Figure 5-1 illustrates the Chan-

Fig. 5-1. Exercise 54: some chancery cursive letters differ from Italics.

cery Cursive letters that differ from those of Practical Italics. Practice writing a few rows of each letter, until each feels comfortable. Notice how few changes you will have to make to learn the Chancery Cursive alphabet.

Exercise 55. This exercise will help you to become familiar with the entire Chancery Cursive alphabet (Fig. 5-2). Write the alphabet a few times while thinking about the differences from Practical Italics.

Simple majuscules, such as those you learned in Chapter 4 for use with Practical Italics minuscules, can be used with Chancery Cursive letters. You can instead choose the slightly more complicated flourished capitals which will follow. Let the use of the lettering dictate which type of capitals to employ.

Remember that there is even more freedom in the formation of Italic capitals than in the formation of minuscules. Practice this new style of capitals as well as the one previously presented; then try your own variations.

Exercise 56. Figure 5-3 presents the first six letters of the Chancery Cursive flourished capital alphabet. Follow the arrows for the direction of the strokes. Be free and loose as you make these bold strokes.

Exercise 57. Figure 5-4 illustrates the letters G through L. Practice each letter until it feels familiar

Exercise 58. Figure 5-5 shows how to form the letters M, N, O, P, Q, and R. The tops of these majuscules should be about halfway between the waist and top lines on your practice paper, or about seven pen widths high.

Exercise 59. In this exercise, you will practice the letters S, T, U, and V (Fig. 5-7). Check to see that your letters are at the correct 5- to 10-degree right-hand slant.

Exercise 60. Figure 5-7 presents the last four letters of the alphabet: W, X, Y, and Z. Notice and copy the slight curve of the W and the wavy top and bottom lines of the Z.

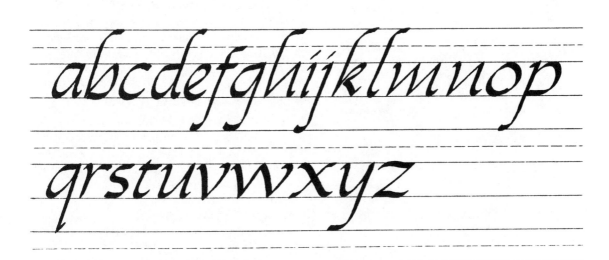

Fig. 5-2. Exercise 55: become familiar with the Chancery Cursive alphabet.

Fig. 5-3. Exercise 56: the first six letters.

Fig. 5-4. Exercise 57: G through L.

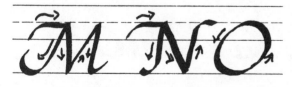

Fig. 5-5. Exercise 58: make the M through the R.

Fig. 5-6. Exercise 59: practice S, T, U, and V.

Fig. 5-7. Exercise 60: the last four letters.

Once you have practiced these capital letters, you can begin to experiment and find your own style. You may decide to develop several different styles of capitals for use on different occasions. Altering your capitals can give an entirely different look to your writing.

JOINING CHANCERY CURSIVE LETTERS

Chancery Cursive lettering is used as a formal hand; therefore it is often not connected. There may, however, be instances when you want the formality of Chancery Cursive, but you do want it connected. Even then there will be many letters that do not connect gracefully. Remember that when you use Chancery Cursive lettering, beauty is the main objective; do not connect the letters just because it is faster.

The same basic lettering theory applies that you used in joining Practical Italic letters. Lift your pen slightly when joining to keep the lines light and thin. Try different ways of joining letters; then consistently use the ones that suit you best.

Letters are divided into the same three groups for joining as were used for Practical Italic letters. Group one consists of letters that end on the upstroke: a, c, d, h, i, k, l, m, and u. Group two includes letters that begin on the upstroke: i, m, n, p, r, t, u, v, w, x, and y. Group three is made up of letters that are joined with previous letters by causing them to just touch on the way down.

The letter b is almost never joined to another letter, and the letter r joins better with letters that come before it than with those that come after it. The letter s can appear joined when it is followed by a letter from the first group. The letters v, w, x, and z are best joined only at the beginning of a stroke. Lift your pen and cross the t and f before you join them to the letters that follow them. Often it is best not to join them to the next letter.

Do not join b, l, h, or k to previous letters, but l, h, and k can be joined to letters that follow. The letter o often can stand alone, but sometimes you can link it to letters that precede or follow it with a horizontal join.

Most letters are joined with either the horizontal or diagonal line. To join letters from group one to letters from group two, simply continue the upstroke of the first letter until it becomes the downstroke of the letter from group two that follows it.

If any of this discussion is difficult or unclear, return to the section on joining Practical Italics letters in Chapter 4. The guidelines are the same. Practice joining letters using sentences that use most, or all, of the letters in the alphabet. A familiar one is: A quick brown fox jumps over the lazy dog.

Practice different ways of joining letters and develop your own style. Remember that not all letters will join well. If you are in doubt about a join, do not use one.

A WORD ABOUT PUNCTUATION

You are ready to use calligraphy in almost any place that you write. You have learned minuscule and majuscule Practical Italics and minuscule and

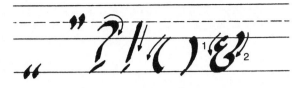

Fig. 5-8. Punctuation.

majuscule Chancery Cursive Italics. Now you need some punctuation, abbreviation, and word division guidelines.

Punctuation marks should be clear and bold (Fig. 5-8). Question marks, quotation marks, and exclamation marks are penned the same height as the majuscules used in the text. Parentheses and ampersands correspond in height to the minuscule ascenders. All normal punctuation and grammar rules govern manuscripts drawn in calligraphy. The clarity of the message is of utmost importance.

One use of abbreviations, other than the accepted Mr., Mrs., Ms., Dr., etc., should be avoided in calligraphy, except when using Practical Italics for casual writing.

If at all possible, do not divide a word at the end of a line. Later in this book you will learn about line finishers and how to use them to fill space at the end of a short line. Never divide proper names, dates, or places. When it is unavoidable, make a clear, recognizable hyphen. When you do divide a word, be sure to make the break between syllables.

Paragraphing should also follow normal English usage rules. Shorter paragraphs are more inviting to read, and it is best if there is a variety of paragraph lengths. It makes the text look more interesting.

When you are penning a formal piece of calligraphy where precision is vital, try a special breathing trick used by professional calligraphers. Simply hold your breath while writing. Breath deeply between words, at the end of the line, before you cross your t's and f's, and before you dot your i's. In other words, breathe any time you lift your pen. Do not breathe while your pen is touching the paper.

Although this breathing technique may sound awkward and difficult, it will become natural if you practice often. It does make conversation nearly impossible, but you should be concentrating on your calligraphy anyway.

NUMBERS

As you use your calligraphy, you will often need to use numbers. Numbers used with the Practical Italics should be kept simple and easy to read. Numbers used with Chancery Cursive can be more decorative.

Exercise 61. Figure 5-9 gives an example of a clean, easy-to-read and easy-to-write set of numbers. Practice them in different sequences until all are comfortable for your hand.

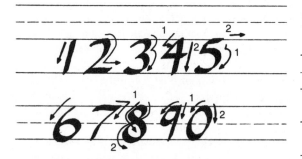

Fig. 5-9. Exercise 61: easy-to-read numbers.

Exercise 62. Figure 5-10 presents a more ornate set of numbers, suitable for use with Chancery Cursive Italics.

Use the counter system to make sure that your

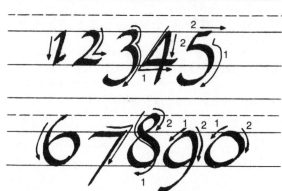

Fig. 5-10. Exercise 62: more ornate numbers.

numbers are being drawn in the correct proportions. The widest part of each number should almost touch the widest part of the next number.

LETTER VARIATIONS

The Italic alphabets, while retaining the classic Roman look, offer the calligrapher the opportunity to be creative even in letter formation.

Exercise 63. A standard variation on the letter e is explained in Fig. 5-11. The e presented in your original Practical Italic and Chancery Cursive alphabets was penned in one stroke. This variation is drawn with two strokes. The first stroke nearly duplicates the letter c, and the second stroke begins at the waist line and curves to the right and back to the original stroke about halfway down toward the base line.

Fig. 5-11. Exercise 63: a variation of the e.

Exercise 64. The letter s can also be modified into a form that is often easier to join with other letters. It is a form that is probably familiar from your own previous style of handwriting. Figure 5-12 illustrates the changed s.

When using Practical Italics for casual com-

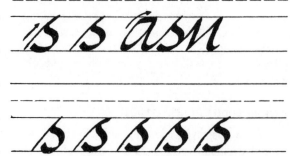

Fig. 5-12. Exercise 64: the letter s can be modified.

munications, many calligraphers leave out not only the bends at the tops of ascenders, but also the bends at the bottoms of the descenders. The alphabet becomes even more efficient then.

Exercise 65. Repeat the descenders in Fig. 5-13 several times before you decide which method you wish to use. The descenders f, g, j, p, q, and y are flexible and look attractive with the clean, straight lines shown in this exercise, or with the bends employed in earlier exercises.

Fig. 5-13. Exercise 65: practice these descenders.

Practice your calligraphy with all of the methods taught in this book and try variations of Italic letters that you see used elsewhere or that you create with your pen and paper. Experiment with all kinds of combinations of letters and joins until you feel ready to decide on your own personal choices. Then be consistent; you will have created your own unique style of beautiful handwriting.

When creating your style of handwriting, follow your instincts. The instructions in this book are only guidelines. If something does not feel comfortable to you after giving it a fair try, substitute your own method.

USING YOUR CALLIGRAPHY

You have the knowledge now to do a great many things with calligraphy. You have practiced two sets of letters: Chancery Cursive and Practical Italics; and you have just become familiar with numbers suitable for use with each alphabet.

Use that knowledge. Actually using your calligraphy skills is the best way to further them. When you use calligraphy to address envelopes, you will be concentrating on correct letter formation, proportion, and spacing. You will judge where

to place the address on the envelope for the most attractive appearance. You will begin to see how to plan a calligraphy manuscript.

While you are practicing your calligraphy by using it in a variety of situations on different kinds of paper, you will be training your most valuable calligraphy aid: your eyes. As you produce early calligraphy projects, you will probably rely heavily on measuring instruments to show you where to place different parts of the manuscript so you end up with a balanced product.

The more you practice, however, the more you will trust your eyes. You will learn to judge how to achieve a balanced look without measuring, but it will only come with a lot of practice.

Although you now understand the theory of Italics and can write both alphabets and numbers, it is best if you continue with a regular practice schedule in addition to using your calligraphy whenever you write.

REVISING YOUR PRACTICE TECHNIQUES

Keep practicing on a regular schedule, but now you should review your practice techniques and perhaps implement some revisions. Your knowledge and skills have grown considerably, and you should now be more critical of your calligraphy.

As always, come to your calligraphy practice session relaxed. Remember to start with clean hands and plenty of inexpensive practice paper.

Start your practice with the loosening-up exercises you learned in Chapter 1. These exercises serve to warm your hand up to calligraphy and transition your mind from everyday cares to the concentration you need to study and practice calligraphy. To help achieve that level of concentration, avoid practicing in a noisy area and avoid conversation. Background music, however, may be beneficial.

Once you have completed the loosening-up exercises, critically evaluate the products of your last practice session—not calligraphy you have done in everyday writing, but calligraphy you executed in your last formal practice session. You can evaluate your calligraphy from two different perspectives: close up to examine details, and from a distance to judge the overall appearance.

From one foot away, critically eye your handwriting for correct letter formation, proportion, and spacing. Compare your letters to those in the exercises in this book. They should be nearly identical, unless you have made a deliberate deviation from the alphabets presented. Use the counter system to determine whether or not your letters are proportional and to check the spacing between letters. Actually draw in a number of counters at various places throughout your practice sheet. When you do find something that needs extra attention, mark it in red.

Next, stand back about 10 feet away from your paper and look at the overall image projected by your calligraphy. Notice the proportion of black lettering to white, or negative, space. Does the writing appear too dense? Are there generous margins at the sides, top, and bottom of the page? What is your impression of the total look? Is it neat, clean, and crisp? This critique of your calligraphy is not vital when you are practicing letters, words, and alphabetic sentences. It will, however, be very useful when you are practicing projects, such as a familiar quote or piece of poetry for a wall hanging.

Once you have critically evaluated your calligraphy from close up and from a distance, your practice can begin. Start by practicing any letters that were not well formed. Take plenty of time, and work on each letter until it is acceptable; then work

on any joins or combinations of letters that were difficult.

This part of your practice may take up most, or all, of your alloted time; it is worthwhile. If you catch and correct poorly formed letters now, you will save extra work later.

Once you have worked on any problem areas, continue your practice session by penning the alphabet several times. You know four alphabets; practice each one.

After completing the alphabets, practice by writing various words. Be sure to use a word list that includes all the letters of the alphabet, including the q, x, and z. Words such as queen, quilt, tranquil, xylophone, extra, zebra, zero, and zesty will help you to practice those infrequently appearing letters.

Use sentences, also. The following sentences use all the letters of the alphabet:

- The quick brown fox jumps over the lazy dog (Fig. 5-14).
- The wizard jumps quickly over eleven green boxes (Fig. 5-15).
- Barking with zeal, the vixen jumped on her foe quickly.
- In the woven zipper bag, Jack's man found exactly a quarter.

Make up your own zany alphabetic sentences to add variety to your repetitious practice. By using several alphabetical sentences you will work on all

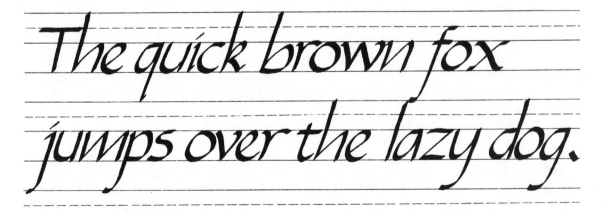

Fig. 5-14. A typical project sample.

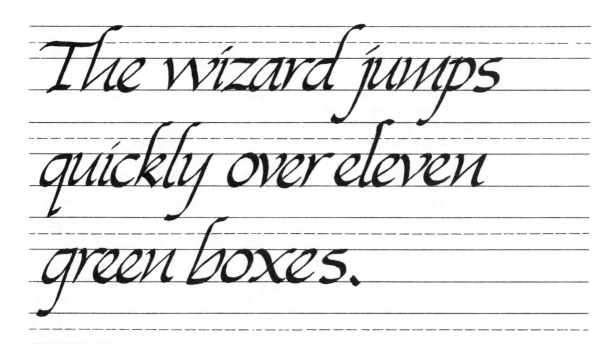

Fig. 5-15. A project sample.

the letters and many letter combinations.

If you would like, finish up your practice time by copying a favorite quotation or poem. Use a clean sheet of practice paper and try to position your quote or poem so that it looks attractive on the paper.

During your practice sessions, periodically check to see that you are sitting in the calligrapher's posture and holding your pen correctly. Be sure to take a break from your practice whenever you begin to feel tense or tired. If taking a break does not ease the tension or tiredness, it is time to quit for the day. You will not make progress, and only become frustrated, if you persist in studying and practicing when you are tired or tense.

If you have not yet changed to a calligraphy fountain pen, now would be a good time to do so. You are by now comfortable with using a chisel tip, and the letter formations are familiar. If you are ready to switch, return to Chapter 3 and read again the description of a calligraphy fountain pen and how to use one. Do some extra practice in order to become acquainted with your new pen.

As you continue to practice calligraphy, save

some of your best work for later review and comparison. If you have saved earlier work, take that out now and compare it with your current calligraphy. Your marked improvement should be motivation to continue with your studies.

Fluency in your calligraphic handwriting will come with time. Your hand, shoulder, and arm will learn to automatically move correctly to create the letters that your brain dictates. The more you write, the sooner that fluency will surface.

MORE WAYS TO IMPROVE YOUR CALLIGRAPHY

Now that you have a firm grasp of the basics of calligraphy and Italics in particular, it may be time to consider taking a class in calligraphy. Classes are offered in many places. All cities and large towns will have calligraphy classes, and even many small towns or rural areas have possibilities.

Calligraphy classes are offered by most colleges, including many community colleges. Often community schools or centers and YMCAs or YWCAs include classes in calligraphy. Also check in your yellow pages under calligraphy, art, and crafts and call your chamber of commerce. Sometimes art stores or art centers offer classes. Ask at your library.

Another way to learn more about calligraphy is through the many books available on the subject. Look them over and study the techniques that interest you. Use books to study the master calligraphers through the ages, too. Your library probably has books on both modern calligraphy and how to learn it, and biographies of master calligraphers with beautiful illustrations of their exceptional work.

You can learn a great deal by studying those illustrations. Look at the letter bodies. Notice the proportions and the precision with which all letters are drawn. Check the percentage of white space to black lettering. Study how the text is arranged on the page. Look at how the manuscript is flourished. Spend a few minutes studying each illustration with your new calligrapher's eye, and you will be surprised at how much you understand of the artist's planning and how he created his work of art. You will see how your new craft can be used to create truly beautiful pieces of art.

Now that you are well into your studies of calligraphy, you may want to talk to others about the subject, compare techniques, and share experiences and knowledge. There may be a calligraphy group in your area. To find out if there is a group, again check your phone book's yellow pages, under organizations and associations. Check the library; call the chamber of commerce; ask at the nearest college or university, community center, or YMCA or YWCA, and talk to people. Someone you know may be a member of a calligraphy group, or have a friend who is a member.

If there is no calligraphy group in your area, think about starting one. If you want to start one, you can reach interested people through an ad in the classified section of your newspaper or shopper and with notices on bulletin boards. Again ask the library, chamber of commerce, college, community center, and others to circulate the information. Once the word is out, and you have a few interested people, set up an organizational meeting and publicize it well. At the meeting, you can discuss the purpose and function of the group, how often to meet, and what type of organizational structure should be used.

You are a calligrapher. Use your skills in many ways, keep on learning, and share your interest with others. The guidelines in Chapter 6 will help you set up a calligraphy studio in your home.

6.
Setting Up
Your Studio

By now you are ready to move your calligraphy work area off the dining room table and to a more permanent and comfortable location. Certainly there is no reason to leave the dining room table if it is working well for you. If, however, you are becoming frustrated with a lack of space, poor lighting, the wrong slant to the surface, or the necessity of clearing your work space for every meal, it is time to look around your home again and find a new location for your calligraphy.

LOCATING YOUR STUDIO

Most homes offer several options for a small calligraphy study or work area. After experimenting with your calligraphy, you are now better equipped to evaluate your needs and your available space in order to design a comfortable, permanent calligraphy space that will not interfere with other aspects of your family life.

Calligraphers work in the living room, family room, bedroom, spare room, and other corners of their living space. They also develop new work spaces in their attics, basements, garages, and even in recreational vehicles, barns, and porches.

While one calligrapher is happy using his or her skill occasionally at the dining room table to address Christmas cards, birthday cards, and invitations, another calligrapher will develop both the talent and ambition to become a professional, complete with expensive studio needs and desires. Most likely your requirements will fall somewhere in between. The location, furnishings, and materials for your studio will reflect your own personal goals, talents, and style.

Living/Family Room. Many families find that they do not fully use both their living and family rooms. If your family tends to use just the family room, consider setting up your calligraphy studio in a corner of the living room. If your needs are modest, a neat work area can be tucked away in a corner without causing any difficulties. Your calligraphy career may be such that all of your needs would fit easily into an attractive desk that would also be a beautiful addition to your furnishings.

If your family room is large, it may be the perfect work space for a desk or drafting table, as well as a file and cabinet for storage. The family's pool table can possibly be relocated to the garage, and the sewing machine can be moved into the bedroom. Don't overlook the possibility of rearranging furniture and activities to help accommodate your new craft.

Bedroom. Some bedrooms are too tiny to house more than a bed and dresser; many, however, are more spacious. Often that space is left vacant. A bedroom calligraphy studio offers privacy, quiet, and a door to shut away the clutter when you are in the middle of a project. Depending on its size and your calligraphy needs, your bedroom could offer a viable alternative as a work space.

Spare Room. A lucky few calligraphers have a spare room in their home just waiting to be used. If you fall into this category, take full advantage of your good fortune and set up the studio of your dream, as far as your budget allows. Since you have the space available, try to anticipate your needs for a few years ahead. Allow a little extra space everywhere and purchase a little better quality calligraphy furnishings and materials than you currently need. It will pay off in the long run because you will be satisfied with your work area for years to come.

Sometimes the term "spare room" is used very loosely. Your spare room may already be used for a number of things such as sewing, ironing, and crafts, and may even double as a guest room. Don't be discouraged. Decide which items you really need in the room and move the rest to the attic, garage, family room, or other appropriate space. You may have opened enough room to easily house your calligraphy equipment.

Creating Space. Wonderful new spaces can sometimes be developed in attics, basements, and garages. A home with an unfinished attic offers endless possibilities. Go up to the attic and turn your imagination loose. The corner next to the chimney may easily be converted into a cozy work space. Attic windows may offer the best lighting in the whole house. Even the atmosphere of the attic

can be an advantage to an artist.

Your basement may also be a candidate for a successful calligraphy studio. A partial or full basement, whether finished or unfinished, can be converted. The cost, of course, will depend on the initial condition of the basement and the details of the finished studio.

Your garage could offer the best site for a studio. Many garages have room to spare with two cars parked and family belongings stored on the shelves. Some framing and a few pieces of plywood can partition off a private calligraphy work space.

Other Spaces. Take a tour of your home and any other structures or possible work sites. You just might come up with a very creative calligraphy studio. A seldom-used motor home or travel trailer can make a comfortable, attractive work area. Many of the necessary furnishings are already installed. The dining table may double as a desk; cupboards and drawers present plenty of storage space. A heat system is available and lighting can be easily arranged.

In some climates, the front porch of your home would be a natural setting for a studio. In other climates, a porch can be made habitable year round by enclosing it with glass. A porch offers the feel and attraction of the outdoors even if it is enclosed in glass. Wiring for lighting should be a simple task: in fact natural light may need very little supplementation.

Look around for other unique possibilities. Do you have a barn, boathouse, or storage building? Keep your imagination active as you explore your home for the best location for your calligraphy studio.

PLANNING YOUR STUDIO

After taking a leisurely tour of your home, make a list of the sites that could be made into a calligraphy studio. List all possibilities, then begin to eliminate. You should be left with the best choices.

Now make a list of needs for your space, followed by a list of wants. On the needs list will be items such as adequate lighting, heat, enough work space, storage, and whatever else you consider absolutely necessary. Some calligraphers will require total privacy, while others can work with other activity around them. Be honest in your evaluation of your needs so that you will be happy with your work space.

Your wants list will be even more personal. You might want to have soft background music available or a window with a beautiful view. You might want a space that stays warm in the winter and cool in the summer with little artificial help.

Now it's time to compare your two lists. You want to find the site that has the most of your needs and wants. It is very likely that none of your choices meets all of your needs and wants, but with a few alterations at least one of the choices will make an excellent calligraphy studio.

The area you choose must have sufficient space to house your calligraphy needs, whether it be a small table, drafting table, or large desk, and adequate storage. A too small space will soon feel cramped, and you will be dissatisfied and looking for a new space.

Adequate lighting is also a necessity in every artistic studio. Natural lighting is, of course, best, but artificial lighting can simulate natural lighting very well. Indirect sunlight coming from over your left shoulder is ideal. Be sure to keep this in mind when planning placement of your work surface. A 75- or 100-watt light bulb is the next best lighting. It also should be positioned so that the light falls over your left shoulder to eliminate glare and shadows on your work.

If your intended calligraphy work space has most of your needs and wants, you can quickly and inexpensively equip your studio. If some major items are missing, however, you will want to do a cost analysis before beginning your conversion.

While your attic offers privacy and perfect daylight through a well-placed window, it may lack heat and finished walls. Maybe you can live with the unfinished walls for the time being, but you must have enough heat to keep your fingers nimble. Sometimes heat can be obtained by installing a floor grate to allow heat to rise from the room below. If your studio is to be in a small enclosure, a space heater may provide the inexpensive heat you need.

While searching out your calligraphy studio, remember that in order to produce clean, neat work, you must work in a clean environment. Keep this in mind especially when checking attics, garages, basements, and outbuildings.

As you decide what needs to be done to your calligraphy space, write down the changes that need to be made, and find out how much they will cost. If you or someone in your family is handy with a hammer, conversion may cost little. If no one in your family wants to tackle the job, consider bartering for the services. Maybe the first project out of your new studio can be the creation of a letterhead and business cards for the carpenter who builds your studio.

Also consider your time when you plan your remodeling. If you are a very busy person, it may be worthwhile to contract for the required work. If you like to fix and change in your spare time, by all means do your own conversion. Evenings and weekends for a short time may be all that is needed. Perhaps it can be a family project. Children like to fetch and help paint; older ones can do some of the carpentry, and your spouse may want to be involved.

FURNISHING YOUR STUDIO

The furniture you choose will depend on your talents and taste. Your work surface is the most important item to consider. By now you have acquired personal preferences. Do you need a properly slanted writing surface, or is a flat desk best for you? Calligraphers use tables, drafting tables, portable drafting tables, desks, and homemade surfaces. Whatever works best for you is what you should use.

You will probably need to augment the storage space in your potential studio site. You can build in storage cabinets or purchase freestanding cabinets at a hardware or department store. You may also want to purchase a two- or four-drawer file cabinet so you can keep track of projects. The cabinet, of course, will be used for keeping supplies, including papers, ink, frames, and others.

A comfortable chair is essential; a secretarial chair is a good choice. You must be able to sit with your back straight, at the proper angle to the writing surface.

If you intend to have clients in your studio, you will need additional seating, which can be anything from a straight back chair to an easy chair.

Decorate your studio with samples of your own calligraphy as well as that of others, including reproductions of professional calligraphy. Keep in mind your goals for your calligraphy career as you decorate. If you want to just use your calligraphy casually, collect samples of greeting cards and invitations that you like and tack them on the walls. If you want to specialize in business cards, decorate with them. If you like, decorate with calligraphy wall hangings, or whatever inspires you. Make your studio as unique as your calligraphy; both are an expression of yourself.

SUPPLYING YOUR STUDIO

Your studio can be supplied with a minimum of materials at this point and added to as the need arises. Right from the beginning, however, there are several items you will want to have on hand. The first consideration is your basic tool—your calligraphy pen. You may still be working with a felt-tip pen with a chisel point, or you may have advanced to a professional Mitchell calligraphy pen.

The Calligraphy Nib Pen

Many professional calligraphers depend on the Mitchell pen as the foundation of their calligraphy studio. At this point in your training, you may be ready to experiment with this true calligrapher's tool.

The Mitchell pen (Fig. 6-1), as well as other professional calligraphy pens (Fig. 6-2) differs from the fountain pen in that it is designed to use India ink. *India ink* is waterproof, permanent ink. It can only be used in a pen that is disassembled and cleaned following each use. If left in a pen, India ink will dry up and ruin the nib.

The Mitchell pen consists of a wooden or plastic shaft with a brass collar and a reservoir nib holder with a detachable steel nib (Fig. 6-3). Before the pen is used for the first time, the light layer of oil applied to the nib by the manufacturer to keep the nib dry must be removed. The oil can be removed by either washing the nib with soap and water or by sucking on the nib. Next, flex the reservoir slightly and slide the nib between the

Fig. 6-1. Mitchell-type pen.

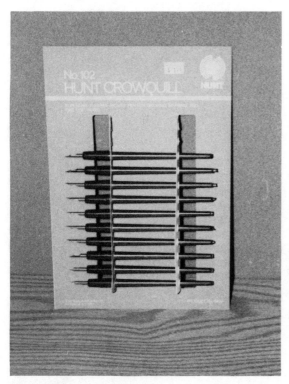

Fig. 6-2. Professional calligraphy pens.

minute, it should be emptied. If ink is left in the pen, it will dry to a crust, and an accumulated crust will quickly ruin the pen by pushing the nib open at the slit, which will alter the ink flow and the nib width.

To empty the pen for a short time between uses, lay it nib side down on a folded tissue, clean rag, or damp tea bag. When you are ready for it again, simply refill it. When you are finished with the pen for the session, blot out the ink that remains in the pen with a tissue and then disassemble and rinse the nib and reservoir.

Other good broad-edged pens which resemble the quill pen, are manufactured by Speedball, Pelikan, Heintze and Blanckert, and Boxall. These pens vary somewhat in shape, range of nib widths, and reservoir design, but all perform the same function. All draw the thick and thin strokes required in calligraphy.

India ink may be used with all of these pens. Some calligraphers find India ink too dense, and opt for another type, such as Higgins General Drawing Ink. When colored inks are required, Dr. Martin's and Luma bottled water-based dye are good choices. Many colors are available, and they produce a luminous quality.

As always, the key is a lot of practice to become familiar with the new tools and materials. If you wish to create calligraphy projects that endure over many years, you will need to become competent with the calligraphy nib pen and permanent inks. Permanent ink cannot be used in your calligraphy fountain pen, because it will clog and ruin it.

Whatever your preference, be sure to have enough pens on hand so that you do not have to pause in the middle of a project to make a trip to the art supply store for a new pen or tip. This may also be the time to branch out and try a variety of pens. Like most calligraphers, you might discover that you like one type of pen for one project, and another type of pen for another project.

Other Writing Tools

Be sure to keep your pens stored in a dry, clean place so they will always be ready to use and will not be harmed by dried ink.

You will also need several sharp pencils, eras-

layers of the collar.

The pen can be filled either of two ways, by dipping or with a dropper. To fill by dipping, simply immerse the nib in India ink to cover the hole and wipe off any extra ink. To fill with a dropper, put just one drop of ink onto the hole in the nib and tap the pen lightly until the drop of ink runs into the pen reservoir. By filling the pen with a dropper you know exactly how much ink is in the pen and you begin your work with a clean nib tip.

Go ahead and try your pen now. After you have used it a few minutes, check to see that you are using it correctly and that the ink is flowing properly. Make several straight downward strokes. Too much ink coming over or under the nib rather than flowing from the center hole causes ink blobs on the paper. To correct this situation, wipe the excess ink off the pen before writing and be sure the ink drop flows into the reservoir.

Never let the ink dry up in your Mitchell pen. If you will not be writing with your pen within one

Fig. 6-3. An assortment of steel nibs.

ers, and a good pencil sharpener to plan and mark your calligraphy paper. If you are adventurous, add a variety of paint brushes to your shopping list. Some calligraphy jobs will call for brushes, rather than pens, for execution. Practice working with them, and your skills will be broadened considerably. If you wish to get into sign painting, you will need skills with paint brushes.

Other Calligraphy Needs

Other tools useful to the calligrapher include rulers, guides, curves, protractors, scissors, glue, tacks, tape, and other assorted art supplies. You may add frames, mounting boards, and other miscellaneous items. Your particular needs and choices will become evident as your calligraphy career advances.

Papers are again a matter of choice; the most popular are lined notebook paper, unlined typing paper, graph paper, and drafting paper for the beginner. As you continue, you will advance to fancier papers, including bristol board and other rag content papers, poster board, and other appropriate papers.

Storage of Supplies

The storage of your paper supply is important. Paper should be stored flat on shelves large enough to accommodate the entire piece of paper. If possible, store paper in its original container until you need it. If paper is allowed to become damp, it will warp and curl, becoming nearly impossible to use for calligraphy. If you invest in a variety of papers, you will be able to attempt nearly any calligraphy project you wish. Of course, you can also add to your paper supplies at any time.

In addition to the all-purpose black Higgins General Drawing Ink, you may want to experiment with a variety of mediums. Browse through the calligraphy section of your favorite art store and try a new ink or paint periodically. Don't buy more ink than you can use in a reasonable amount of time, however. Always store your ink in tightly closed containers; Storage in a dark cabinet will also slow deterioration of color and consistency.

When you are finished you should have the calligraphy studio or work area of your dreams. It will be uniquely yours, an expression of your artistic ability and your personality.

WHAT'S COMING NEXT

Now that you have learned four calligraphy alphabets and are familiar with many calligraphy tools and types of materials, you are ready to produce your first calligraphy project.

Chapter 7 will take you step by step through the planning, designing, and executing of a creative piece of calligraphy. You will choose a quote or poem, decide on page layout, choose a calligraphy style, design a border, create a handline, and finally begin work on your first calligraphy creation.

7.

Planning

Calligraphy Projects

You now have the penmanship skills necessary to create a beautiful piece of calligraphy. You may even have been asked by a friend or civic group to design and produce a sign, bulletin, or invitation. You can do it. This chapter will take you through the step-by-step process of planning and creating a wall hanging for your own home. The process can be adapted to many other calligraphy projects.

PROJECT IDEAS

Calligraphy can be used anywhere that handwriting is used, and in many instances it can also be used in place of typography. The many places you can use calligraphy include announcements, quotations, personal letterheads, poetry, invitations, greeting cards, and family trees (Fig. 7-1).

Announcements and invitations can be warmly personal if they are lovingly designed and penned (Fig. 7-2). They can give the appearance of being individually created if you make an original and have it professionally printed. Modern printing facilities can produce top quality reproductions on your choice of papers at a reasonable cost. If you have time, it is wonderful practice to actually write each separate announcement or invitation. Greeting cards (Fig. 7-3) can also be done in this fashion.

Design your own personal stationery (Fig. 7-4). Make it elegant or casual, depending on your correspondence. You could also design two, one for personal letters and one for business. You can also make matching business cards.

A family tree would make a cherished gift for a loved relative or as an addition to your own home. It can be small and simple, beginning with your parents or grandparents, or it can be large and complex, tracing your ancestors back generations before they crossed the Atlantic.

The most popular calligraphy project is the handlettered favorite quotation or piece of poetry (Fig. 7-5). A simple quote or short poem is an excellent first calligraphy project because it can be easily planned and quickly completed. As with any learning process, it is best to begin with an easy task and work up to more complicated work.

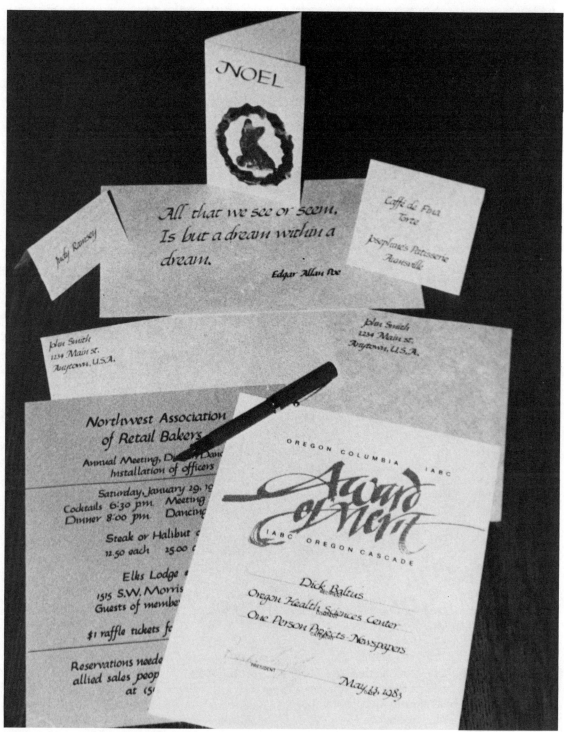

Fig. 7-1. Typical calligraphy projects.

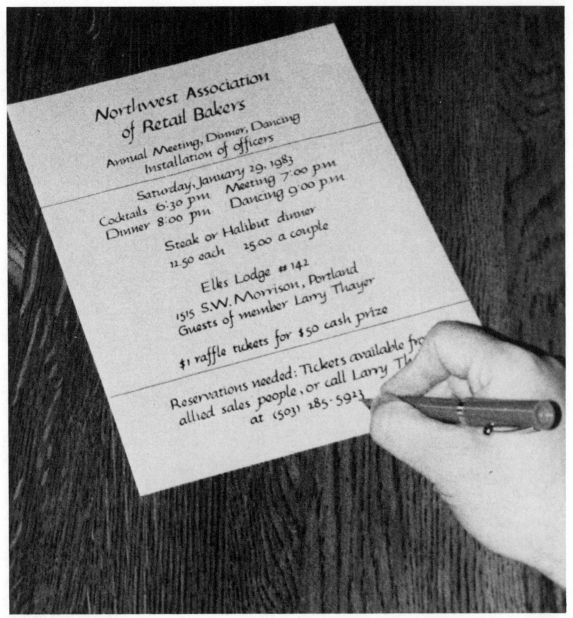

Fig. 7-2. Announcement.

Use your own favorite quotation or choose from the following list. Look at this project as a learning exercise, and if it turns out well you will have a special gift or new decoration for your home. Here are some possible quotations:

- *I never met a man I didn't like.* Will Rogers
- *All that we see or seem Is but a dream within a dream.* Edgar Allan Poe
- *The soul of man is immortal and imperishable.* Plato
- *Nothing is so firmly believed as what we least know.* Michel de Montaigne

Fig. 7-3. Greeting card.

- *He is now fast rising from affluence to poverty.* Mark Twain
- *Cauliflower is nothing but cabbage with a college education.* Mark Twain

Many favorite quotations are taken from the Hole Bible. The following are all from *The Living Bible.*

- *For God loved the world so much that he gave his only Son so that anyone who believes in him shall not perish but have eternal life.* John 3:16
- *Look! I have been standing at the door and I am constantly knocking. If anyone hears me calling him and opens the door, I will come in and fellowship with him and he with me.* Revelation 3:20
- *O Lord, I will praise you with all my heart, and tell everyone about the marvelous things you do.* Psalms 9:1

- *In your day of trouble, May the Lord be with you!* Psalms 20:1
- *Because The Lord is my Shepherd, I have everything I need!* Psalms 23:1

If one of these quotations does not inspire you, and you have none other in mind, thumb through *Bartlett's Familiar Quotations* or your Bible, and you will find many quotations and poems worth preserving. You can also make up your own phrase or poem for an original piece of art.

To follow through on a project, throughout this chapter the quotation "All that we see or seem, Is but a dream within a dream," will be used.

PLANNING YOUR PROJECT

Your first calligraphy project should be kept simple. Choose a short quotation and plan a simple design using only black ink on good quality paper. Later in your calligraphy career, you will have to choose whether or not to use other colors and in what medium. The use of colors will be briefly discussed in Chapter 8.

Since you are using only two styles of Italic writing, the choice should be easy. You will probably decide on Chancery Cursive for this project, since it is an attempt at formal calligraphy. If you have become familiar with the true calligrapher's pen and nibs, use them for your finished product. Your calligraphy fountain pen will also do a satisfactory job.

Next comes the main part of planning your project: designing the layout of the page. The *layout* is how the page will be put together; it is a rough plan showing the arrangement of all parts of a design. It can be considered a floor plan for the finished product.

As you make your layout, you must consider all the elements that will be present in the finished project, including the text, any illustrations, margins, white space, a headline if appropriate, borders, and line finishers. Since this is a creative process, all decisions are subjective and will reflect your personality and judgment. Follow your own inclinations.

Your first decisions are general ones, such as the image you wish to project. Try to visualize the

Fig. 7-4. Letterhead and envelope.

layout in your mind. Your job now is to transfer that image in your mind onto paper. Do you want your piece of artwork to appear elegant or casual, simple or ornate? Is the content of the message the most important factor, or is the appearance of primary interest? All of these things will influence your design.

Do you intend to incorporate an illustration or a design into your project? Do you visualize a border surrounding the text or simple white margins?

The easiest project to begin with is a simple quotation or very short poem that will be centered on the page, without illustration and with a very simple border, if any. A heading or title is not necessary on a quotation but may enhance a poem. It is always appropriate to give credit to the author by penning his name at the end of the text. For the short quote, no line finishings will be necessary, but for some poems, line finishings may be used to achieve a balanced look to the text.

Now that you have considered all the elements of your project and have a visualization of it in your head, it is time to transfer that image onto paper, first with pencil as a blueprint, and eventually with your calligraphy pen and ink.

In addition to your calligraphy pen, the tools and materials you will need for this first project are minimal. You will need rough draft paper (inexpensive typing paper will do nicely), pencils, an eraser, a ruler, and good paper for the finished product.

For this piece of calligraphy, and for many to come, you may wish to purchase a special calligraphy paper that is available at stationery, art, and some variety stores. If you want to use a higher quality paper, both the Bainbridge and Strathmore companies offer good quality 100% rag bristol board in five different thicknesses. This is a good, all-purpose calligraphy paper. As your skills increase, and your calligraphy projects become more ambitious, you will want to experiment with many different types of writing surfaces, including handmade paper. These, as well as other advanced tools and materials, will be presented in Chapter 8.

PUTTING YOUR IDEAS ON PAPER

Sketch out a rough draft, or layout, of your intended piece of calligraphy. You might make several layouts, especially when you move on to more complex projects, before you are satisfied and ready to begin the actual lettering

Fig. 7-5. Framed quotation.

The Rough Drafts

To make a layout for "All that we see or seem, Is but a dream within a dream" (Fig. 7-6) I first determined approximately how much space the text and any embellishments would occupy. I decided to use the text alone, with no title, no illustrations, a simple line finishing, and a simple border. I gave credit to the author by penning his name under the quotation. Since the content of the message is the most important element, the design should not overpower the message. A simple, clean, straight-forward design best conveys the meaning. Wishing this to be more than a casual communication, however, I used the Chancery Cursive mode of Italic handwriting.

When all of these decisions had been made, I was ready to transfer the image in my head onto my rough draft paper. I intended to have my finished product on a piece of 8½-×-11-inch standard calligraphy paper. Plenty of white space conveys simplicity and elegance to me, so used wide margins.

There are three styles of margins used most often. One option is to have equal margins on all four sides of the text. Another is to have the top and bottom margins equal but larger than the side margins, which are also equal. The third option, and the most popular, is to have the sides and top equal, but the bottom margin obviously larger. I chose to use the third option.

Since my quotation was extremely short and I chose to use no illustrations and only a simple border, the layout was quite easy. My next decision was whether to use the paper lengthwise or to use its width. To decide, I quickly sketched my planned project on a piece of practice paper using both methods. For this quotation, I chose to use the paper on its width.

The technique of quickly sketching your ideas onto practice paper is useful in making many decisions about your final layout. A good way to plan your project is to make a list of proposed elements, and then sketch them out in many different patterns to determine which methods you prefer. You may change your design several times while experimenting. Keep on trying until you think you have the best possible layout that will help create a piece of calligraphy which will impart your message both intellectually and visually.

Since I was using such a short quotation, I needed to take care that my page not look empty. Too much white space can detract from the message and aesthetics as much as can a crowded appearance. With my short quote, I could change my mind and decide to use a smaller finished size. If I were penning a long quotation that looked crowded on the page, I could opt to use a larger piece of paper. When a great deal of text is involved, it is vital to retain a good-sized margin on all sides to avoid a crowded look.

Justification and Spacing

After making several sketches of "All that we see or seem, Is but a dream within a dream," I decided that the finished wall hanging should be smaller than the 8½-×-11-inch size I earlier considered. I retained the 11-inch width, but cut the height down to approximately 6 inches.

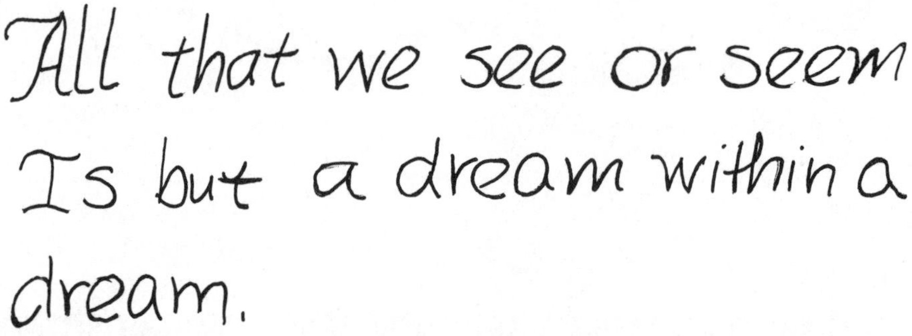

All that we see or seem
Is but a dream within a
dream.

Fig. 7-6. Project's rough sketch.

Again, since my quotation was so short, my layout decisions were easy. Since I had only two lines that are of differing lengths, I did not need to worry about justification. *Justification* is how the lines end, whether they all begin flush at the left margin and end flush at the right margin. Nonjustified writing or printing is said to have *ragged* margins. If you are using a lengthy piece of text, you will need to determine how you want your lines to begin and end, justified or nonjustified. It is much more difficult to make your handlettered lines appear justified on the right margin than it is to allow that margin to be slightly ragged.

Of course it is best to make the lines as nearly as possible the same length, but save the extra difficulty of true justification for later in your calligraphy career. To make the text appear justified, use line finishings, which will be discussed later.

For the purpose of spacing, if your text is lengthy, you will need to know how many characters are in the text. To determine the number of characters, type your copy with your typewriter margins set for 60 characters per line. Then simply multiply the number of characters per line by the number of typed lines.

The next step is to letter a line of the text in the style chosen for the finished work, using the exact letter spacing and letter form and size intended. Make the line the length of the proposed finished line length. Now count the characters in the line, allowing one character between words and two characters between sentences. The line should be flush to the right margin, even if that means stopping in the middle of a word.

Perhaps you counted 45 characters in your single line. Let's say your full text contains 415 characters. Divide 45 into 415 to find a close estimate of how many lines your text will require. In this case it is 9 lines plus a few extra characters. With this information, you can more accurately plan your project and devise a useful layout.

The Final Layout

By now you have chosen the quotation or poem you are going to copy; the lettering style, pen, ink and paper you will use and a rough draft of your layout. Now make a final, precise layout before you attack your final product (Fig. 7-7).

To make this final layout, use either your calligraphy fountain or nib pen or a chisel-tip pen. Any of these can make the layout exactly like your proposed finished piece of artwork. Using your practice paper, lightly mark in pencil the margins you will use, using a ruler for accuracy. Also lightly draw lines so your writing is straight. Next letter in your text and any headlines, forming the letters precisely as you expect to do in your wall hanging. This procedure will ensure that your spacing is

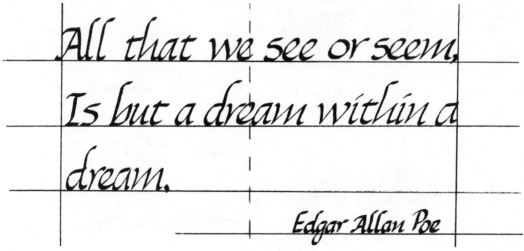

Fig. 7-7. Planning the project.

83

correct and that you have chosen an appropriate lettering style and size.

Line Finishings

If you need to use line finishings to give your manuscript a completed look, be sure to include them in your layout. Your layout should be exactly like your proposed project except for the tools and materials you use. The design should be identical, or it will not give you a true prediction of what your wall hanging will look like when finished.

Line finishings are ornamental designs used to fill those white spaces at the end of a line of writing. They are useful when a word or sentence ends close to the end of a line, but without enough space to accommodate the next word. Blank spaces can also occur at the end of a paragraph or at the end of the text.

If the empty space is minimal, it can likely be filled with a flourish to the end stroke of the last letter of the line. If the space is larger, however, it will require specially designed line finishings. Line finishings should always be drawn with the same pen as used for the text, and they should be unobtrusive. Although line finishings are useful for plugging small white spaces, they should not be used so often that they call attention to themselves.

When you choose a line finishing, consider the style of handwriting that is being used, and match the line finishing to the lettering characteristics. Following are some standard line finishings and how to create them. Try them all and see which you like. Even if you do not intend to use line finishings in your first calligraphy project, this is a good time to become acquainted with them.

Exercise 66. Figure 7-8 illustrates line finishing that is often used. Using your ruled paper and your favorite calligraphy pen—a medium point

nib is still best at this stage—make several lines of the three-dot line finishing. Trace first, if it helps, then draw the finishings freehand. Follow the numbered sequence when making your finishings.

Exercise 67. This exercise takes the dot design of finishings one step further, making a sequence of four dots (Fig. 7-9). Again, follow the numbering for the correct construction of the design.

Fig. 7-9. Exercise 67: a sequence of four dots.

Exercise 68. Figure 7-10 shows one more variation on the dot design. The three dots are stacked vertically with a flourish in each direction from the center dot.

Several other line finishings are illustrated, and their creation is self explanatory (Fig. 7-11).

Fig. 7-10. Exercise 68: another variation.

Fig. 7-11. Sample line finishers.

Fig. 7-8. Exercise 66: line finishing.

Experiment with all and use the one that appeals to you and is best suited for your first calligraphy project. You can also create your own line finishings and study those used in professional calligraphy. As your eye becomes more trained, you will learn a great deal by studying professional and master calligraphers.

Once you have decided on a line finishing style, insert any you need in your layout. Remember to keep their use to a minimum so you do not detract from the text or the overall appearance. Used in moderation, line finishings can enhance a work of calligraphy.

Borders

Borders are often not necessary in calligraphy, especially if the piece is to be framed. When borders are used, they should compliment the lettering style used. When in doubt, simplicity is best. With my quotation I chose an easy-to-do black border. Since I planned to frame it, my wall hanging could be produced attractively without any border.

If you decide a border is necessary to your product, choose one from those illustrated in Fig. 7-12, design your own, or experiment with those you see in other books or on other pieces of calligraphy. At this point your borders should be kept as simple black-line designs. Later in your calligraphy career, you can learn about and use colors in ornate patterns. The border you have chosen should appear on your final layout.

Now that your layout is complete, take an inventory of it. Does it include all of the elements needed to convey the message you wish to communicate? Study your layout from about 1 foot away. Does it appear balanced? Are there too many line finishings? If the line finishings are noticeable, there are probably too many. Is your quotation or poem easy to read? Is there too much white space? Are the margins wide?

Now tack your layout to the wall and stand back about 10 feet for an evaluation. Consider the overall appearance. Does it look like you want it to look? Does the text seem crowded? Does it appear simple and elegant, or warm and inviting? Is it the feeling that you want to convey?

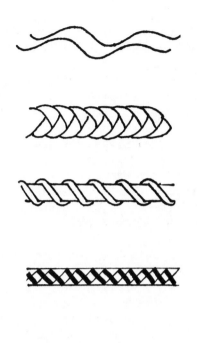

Fig. 7-12. Sample border designs.

Now is the time to make any changes you think would improve your wall hanging. If you are not satisfied with your layout, you will not be satisfied with the final project. If you have any doubts, return to your practice paper. Try changing the part of the layout you are not satisfied with or begin all over again. Extra time in planning will pay off when your final project is produced. If your planning is careful and thorough, the results are almost guaranteed to bring satisfaction.

CREATING YOUR WALL HANGING

You have a layout that you like, and you have the skills to make that layout come alive in a real piece of art: your first true piece of calligraphy.

Preliminaries

You can only produce your best work when you are rested, relaxed, and in the mood to work. Choose a time when your concentration will not be interrupted. Make sure your hands are clean and all your materials are gathered before you start.

As you are working, proceed slowly and cautiously. Stop often to rest. The concentration needed to work on your calligraphy project is demanding. If you find yourself becoming tired or frustrated, stop for the day. Perhaps it will take several sessions to complete your project. Remember that it will endure for many years. A few extra hours invested in its creation will be rewarded many times during the coming years.

Your work area must be tidy and clean. It can be very disheartening to find a smudge on your half-finished project because of a dirty tool, work area, or hands.

Settle in at your desk or table in the comfortable calligrapher's posture and go through a complete session of loosening-up exercises. If you are nervous about your first true calligraphy, do some extra loosening up. It may help to copy your project text once or twice on your practice paper.

When you feel confident you are ready to begin, tack your layout in front of you where you can constantly refer to it. It is your blueprint and can only assist you if you follow it conscientiously.

The first step in the actual execution of your calligraphy is to mark guidelines on your paper very lightly with a soft lead pencil. All guidelines should be drawn as lightly as possible while still being visible.

For easy reference, the first guideline should be a light vertical line down the center of the page. This line will help to keep your page as nearly perfectly balanced as possible. The next task is to mark guidelines for the text, along with any heading. To keep lettering precise and proportioned, four lines are needed for each line of text. They are the base and waist lines, which contain minuscule letter bodies; the top line, which guides ascenders and majuscule letter bodies; and the bottom line, which stops descenders. If these guidelines are drawn carefully, the job of lettering will be simplified.

Lettering Your Wall Hanging

It is time to start lettering. If you have become tense while preparing your writing surface, take a short break and relax. Do a few more loosening-up exercises. Then come back and try a few strokes on a scrap piece of the kind of paper you will use, with the pen you have chosen.

Now go ahead and letter your heading. Doing the large lettering first will serve to further relax your hand before moving on to the small letters of the text. It is perfectly natural to feel tense when beginning a project. Even professional calligraphers often tense up at the start for fear that they will irreparably ruin the writing surface.

While lettering the text, you may need to consciously slow your mind down to correspond with the slow progress of your hand. One of the most common mistakes in lettering is to let your mind to race ahead of your hand, causing the hand to omit letters, words, or entire lines. If the text is lengthy, it may help to cover all but the line on which you are working.

When starting a new line, take care to begin on the correct guideline. In lengthy text with numerous guidelines, it is easy to accidently begin lettering on a line that is meant only to contain descenders, or to begin lettering on the waist line rather than the base line. You can avoid this problem by lightly marking each base guideline with a small asterisk.

If you should make a mistake in lettering your project, unfortunately the best solution is to begin again. Do not become discouraged. The extra practice is incalcuable. All calligraphers make mistakes and have to begin many pieces of art a second, third, or even fifth or sixth time.

After you have completed the heading and text (Fig. 7-13) you will be able to see what your wall hanging is really going to look like. Do critical evaluation like the one you did when your final layout was ready. Does the project live up to your expectations? Does it communicate the message? Is it attractive?

Is there an area that will still appear empty when the design is finished? If so, it can still be added, but be sure that it will add beauty to the manuscript and not look like an afterthought. One way to test is to add the missing element on a very light paper overlay that will allow the original to

All that we see or seem,
Is but a dream within a
dream.

Edgar Allan Poe

Fig. 7-13. Your finished project.

Fig. 7-14. Your next project?

show from below. Any additions at this time should be simple and kept at an absolute minimum.

If there is artwork or ornamentation to be included, transfer it to the original now. Follow your guidelines for accurate placement. Be sure that the lettering ink is thoroughly dried before you apply art, ornamentation, or borders. Allow at least ½ hour after you finish lettering before you again touch the manuscript.

Once any artwork or bordering is completed, again allow the wall hanging to dry thoroughly. Then, very gently, using either a Faber-Castell Magin-Rub eraser or a pointed kneaded eraser, eliminate the guidelines. Erase as little as possible and work slowly and very carefully. Do not erase over your working surface; it must be kept clean. If you erase before the ink has had sufficient time to dry, or if you erase vigorously, you will have disastrous results. Be patient and work gingerly.

The last task in completing your wall hanging is to cut it to its finished size. With your soft lead pencil, lightly mark the finished size on your original piece of art. Then, using a sharp cutting edge, very carfully cut your art to the proper size. An excellent cutting edge is an Olfa utility knife with a sharp blade. A stainless steel ruler makes a good straightedge for the cutting. The cutting tools must be immaculate in order to keep the art clean. A clamp fastened to your table edge will keep your work immobile while you cut. One clean cut should sever most papers. If you are using heavier bristol board, however, two light cuts are more effective than one bold stroke. Be sure to have a backing below your piece of art that will not be harmed by the sharp knife.

Your Finished Project

There it is. Your first calligraphy project. You can frame it if you wish, or hang it on your wall as it is.

Fig. 7-15. Your project can be a colorful story.

First, however, do one more evaluation. Does the piece look finished? Is it crowded? Is there too much white space? Is the message communicated clearly and attractively? Study your calligraphy from about 1 foot away and from about 10 feet away. Be critical but not harsh—it is your first attempt.

Are you satisfied? There will probably be at least a few minor points about your calligraphy that disturb you; that also happens to the professionals. It is always easiest to see what we should have changed after the project is completed.

The important factor is to learn from those things you would change. They will make your next project better. Now that you are finished, it would be good practice to make a new layout of your project, incorporating any changes you think would improve the art.

Plan another project (Fig. 7-14). Keep using your calligraphy. The best practice and the best way to grow is to keep busy. Planning and creating calligraphy art will provide a lot of interesting practice while supplying you with decorations for your home or original gifts for others (Fig. 7-15).

ADVANCING YOUR SKILLS

In Chapter 8 you will learn about a variety of things that will add to your calligraphy skills and knowledge. Advanced materials will be discussed, as well as advanced lettering and ornamenting techniques. The use of colors will be introduced, and you will learn how to make your own calligraphy pen.

8.
Creating
Calligraphy

Paper is, of course, the most commonly used writing surface for calligraphy today. A wide variety of papers that would astound ancient calligraphers is available.

The very best paper is made of either linen or cotton rags and has a neutral pH. The neutral pH means that only a small amount, if any, of chemicals are used, and the paper is neither too acid nor too alkaline. Durable, 100% cotton or linen "rag" paper offers a fine writing surface.

Inexpensive wood-pulp paper is good practice paper, but it lacks the durability and excellent writing surface of rag content paper.

Handmade paper sounds elegant and inviting, but take care when choosing it. The content of the paper is more important than the method of manufacture. If content is equal, the advantage of handmade paper is in its toughness. Machine-made paper has a grain that allows the paper to tear easily in one direction. Handmade papers, on the other hand, are made by a four-way shaking method that makes the fibers interlock from all directions,

creating a stronger paper.

The choice of calligraphy paper naturally depends on the intended use. As explained in Chapter 7, both the Bainbridge and Strathmore companies manufacture a 100% rag content bristol board in several thicknesses. It comes in two finishes, kid and plate. The *plate* finish is a smooth finish, while the *kid* finish is slightly rougher. Many calligraphers prefer the kid finish.

Many manufacturers produce good quality handmade papers. The best way to find the one you like is to experiment with as many as possible.

If a project is to be reproduced, such as an invitation or announcement, expensive rag content paper is not required. Your choice of paper will come at the time of printing.

Explore art shops and stationery stores in your area for the types of paper available. Many stores will have samples of the paper which you can try. Also, talk with other calligraphers who may be interested in sharing a ream of paper. This way you can try a new type of paper without purchasing an entire ream, yet getting the less expensive ream price.

Perhaps the best all-purpose black calligraphy ink is Higgins General Drawing Ink. It is permanent without being thick. Many calligraphers employ India ink, while others find it too thick for use with a calligraphy pen.

Again, within certain limits, the choice is up to you. Experiment with inks until you find those that best suit your individual needs.

MAKING YOUR OWN CALLIGRAPHY PEN

By now you have probably tried several different pens to create your calligraphy: chisel tip, calligraphy fountain pen, and professional calligraphy pen. For a truly unique and personal pen, you can make your own. Two historic types of calligraphy pens are still made by hand today: the reed pen and the quill pen.

The reed pen works best for large writing and is softer than the quill. Quill pens offer smaller, finer writing edges and are hard and dense. Reeds can be found in marshy areas, near water, or in plant stores. Quills can be found at chicken or turkey farms.

The Reed Pen. There are six steps to making a reed into a nib.

- Choose a reed about 8 inches long and obliquely cut off the end, using a very sharp knife.
- About halfway into the first cut, make a second cut toward the writing end. With the knife blade nearly flat to the reed, shave away the inner growth, leaving only the hard outer shell of the reed.
- Place the reed, cut side down, on a very hard surface and cut the top off at a right angle to the shaft.
- To start the slit in the middle of the tip, insert the knife edge at the center of the tip and press lightly.
- The slit must be carefully lengthened. To do so, hold a pencil under the nib while pressing on the top to ensure that the slit does not extend too far. Gently move the handle upward and sideways until the slit is about ¾ inch.

- Again using a hard cutting surface, cut the tip at approximately a 70-degree angle to the pen shaft.

The Quill Pen. Cutting a quill into a nib is a similar operation, but first the quill must be prepared by eliminating the greasy outside membrane and the soft interior pith, called *dutching*, or *clarifying*, the quill.

Dutching, or clarifying, is done by heating the quill over a hot plate. Hold it about 1½ inches above the hot surface and rotate it every 10 seconds to shrivel both the pith and the membrane. Then, holding the quill by the feather end, quickly touch the barrel to the hot plate. Scrape all the film from the barrel with the back edge of a pen knife. After it cools, the quill can be polished with a woolen or linen cloth.

After these steps are completed, the quill can be shaped into a nib in the same way as the reed. The feather barbs should be smoothed away and the shaft cut to about 8 inches. Since the quill is a much harder substance than the reed, it will be more difficult to cut.

The Ink Reservoir. An ink reservoir for either the quill or the reed pen can be fashioned from flexible metal about 2 inches long and cut to the width of the nib. The thin strip of metal is gently curved into an "s" shape. The bottom loop of the metal is placed in the barrel under the nib, creating slight pressure that will hold the reservoir in position. The second loop should be placed about ⅛ inch behind the writing edge in the reed pen. In the quill pen it should be placed about 1/16 inch behind the writing edge. The second loop of the thin strip of metal holds the ink.

That is all it takes to make your own reed quill calligraphy pen. Your handmade pen is uniquely yours. There is not another exactly like it anywhere.

The uniqueness of your handmade pen can cause some difficulties. Since each pen is individually made, you cannot make two pens that produce identical pen strokes. If something happens to your pen in the middle of a project, therefore, you will not have another pen to resort to for completing the project, as you would if you used a standard pen from a major manufacturer.

ROMAN CAPITALS

Roman majuscules are often used in conjunction with other calligraphy styles to adorn a manuscript. They are sometimes illuminated or ornamented at the start of a piece of decorative writing. The following exercises will help you become familiar with Roman Capitals.

A few Roman Capitals are written with the pen at the same 45-degree angle you use for all Italic lettering. These letters are N, V, X, W, and M.

The letters B, C, D, E, F, G, H, I, J, K, L, O, P, Q, R, T, and U are written with the pen held at a 20-degree angle to the paper. To do so, your elbow must be kept near your body.

Both the 45-degree and the 20-degree angles are used in writing the Roman Capitals A, Y, Z, and S.

Exercise 69. Figure 8-1 illustrates the first of six Roman letter families. With your pen at a 20-degree angle, follow the numbered arrows for correct formation of the letters. Notice the I and the backs of the L, E, and F are identical.

Fig. 8-1. Exercise 69: a Roman letter family.

Exercise 70. Figure 8-2 presents four more letters that are formed using a 20-degree angle. The top loop of the letter B is visibly smaller than the bottom loop. Note the flat stroke on the top edge of each letter.

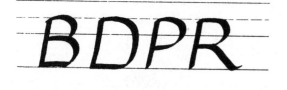

Fig. 8-2. Exercise 70: use a 20-degree angle.

Exercise 71. Figure 8-3 introduces the rounded letters. The O and Q are nearly circular, while the C and G are more egg-shaped. Be sure to follow the numbered arrows for correct formation of the letters. Your pen should again be at the 20-degree angle.

Fig. 8-3. Exercise 71: rounded letters.

Exercise 72. Figure 8-4 illustrates the last family of letters that is drawn entirely with the 20-degree pen angle. The H should be crossed slightly above the middle line.

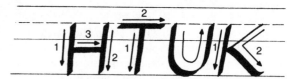

Fig. 8-4. Exercise 72: the last family of letters drawn with a 20-degree angle.

Exercise 73. Figure 8-5 shows how to form the diagonal letters N, X, and V. They are made with a 45-degree pen angle.

Fig. 8-5. Exercise 73: diagonal letters.

Exercise 74. The letters W, J, and M are also made with a 45-degree pen angle. Notice in Fig. 8-6 that the W is wider than the M.

Fig. 8-6. Exercise 74: use a 45-degree angle.

Exercise 75. Figure 8-7 presents the special letters A, Y, Z, and S. All require both the 20-degree and the 45-degree pen angles in their formation. The A, Y, and Z call for the 45-degree pen angle on the horizontal strokes, and the 20-degree angle on the diagonal strokes. The letter S is more complex. Your pen should follow the center curve, with the pen angle always perpendicular to the curve. The 20-degree angle is used on the second and third strokes.

Roman letters are strictly proportioned. The letters O, C, G, Q, and D are exactly as wide as they are tall. The E, F, L, B, P, R, and S are twice as tall as they are wide. The H, T, U, K, N, A, V, J, X, Y, and Z are approximately ¾ as wide as they are tall. Only two letters are wider than they are tall—the M and W are about ¼ wider than they are tall.

Since this is a new lettering style, requiring the use of a new pen angle, some extra practice may be necessary in order to become comfortable with the Roman Capitals.

Fig. 8-7. Exercise 75: special letters.

Exercise 76. Once you are familiar with the entire alphabet, experiment with adding serifs to all letters but the O. An easy, graceful serif that can be used on all the letters is illustrated in Fig. 8-8.

Once they are mastered, these Roman majuscules can be used to beautify many items written in calligraphy. Some short texts may also be appropriate in all Roman Capitals.

Fig. 8-8. Exercise 76: add serifs.

USING COLOR IN CALLIGRAPHY

Colored inks and paint can be used in many ways to enhance a piece of calligraphy. Illuminated letters and ornamental letters are created with color. Many illustrations are done with color. Sometimes colored ink is used for all or part of the text.

During the Middle Ages, calligraphers often hired rubricators to add color to manuscripts. The color offered a transition from the illuminated capitals to the black lettering of the text. The term *rubricate* is still used to mean red writing on a manuscript.

Illuminated letters are letters that are decorated with color or gold. Illuminated letters are larger than letters of the text, but smaller than ornamental letters, which will be discussed later. Fine-point drawing pens, such as the Crowquill Point Brause 66EF, manufactured by Pentalic, are needed for drawing illuminated letters. The best practice paper to use with the drawing pen is good quality drafting paper; inexpensive papers will cause the pen point to become clogged. Also necessary are a few good paintbrushes.

An inexpensive enamel paint that works well for illumination is Testor's Pla Enamel, which is intended for model making. Testor's paint thinner is useful for cleaning brushes.

Exercise 77. This exercise will acquaint you with illuminated letters (Fig. 8-9). Draw a complete alphabet of Roman Capitals, using a draftsman's pencil that is very sharp. Trace over these lines in black ink using your drawing pen.

Exercise 78. Figure 8-10 illustrates a complete set of built-up letters that are nearly ready for illumination. Trace them if you like, then draw them freehand with your draftsman's pencil. Again trace over the lines in black ink with your drawing pen.

Exercise 79. In this exercise, you will add the serifs to the letters to be illuminated. Using the alphabet you made in Exercise 78, add serifs as shown in Fig. 8-11. Lay another piece of drafting paper over this sheet and trace the outline of the letters with your drafting pencil. Remove the bot-

Fig. 8-9. Exercise 77: illuminated letters.

tom sheet and go over the alphabet with your drawing pen.

Exercise 80. In this exercise you will practice drawing illuminated letter outlines freehand. Make your letters look as nearly as possible like the examples in Fig. 8-12.

Exercise 81. In this exercise you can illuminate your alphabet (Fig. 8-13). Shake a bottle of enamel well, dip in your paintbrush and begin. Work with just a small amount of enamel on the brush. When finished with one color, close the bottle tightly and clean the brush with paint thinner and dry it with a paper towel. Try several colors and visualize how they will add to your future calligraphy projects.

When you finish with your paintbrush for the day clean it with paint thinner; then remove all the thinner by washing in dish soap and rinsing.

An *ornamental letter* is a decorated Roman letter that is illuminated and used as the first letter of a portion of text. It is much larger than the text.

Ornamental letters can be created very simply, with just the use of serifs, or complexly, with the incorporation of an elaborate illustration.

Color is used in calligraphy in a number of other ways also. Illustrations that accompany the text on a piece of calligraphy can be all in black, all in one other color, or in two or more colors. If you feel capable of illustrating your own calligraphy, by all means use your artistic talents to add beauty to your projects. If you do not feel capable of creating illustrations that will enhance your text, find a local artist and commission him to illustrate your calligraphy. Perhaps you can work out a trade arrangement where he illustrates your calligraphy and you supply his lettering needs.

Another way in which color is added to a piece of calligraphy is in the use of colored ink for lettering. Color should always be used with caution and in moderation. The variety of colors in different mediums makes it tempting to use many colors often in a variety of ways. Historically, medieval

Fig. 8-10. Exercise 78: a complete set of letters ready for illumination.

scribes generally reserved the use of color for illuminators and rubricators. Color calls attention to itself and can subtract from the overall image. When working with your calligraphy, experiment widely with color, but use it sparingly and carefully on your calligraphy projects.

Jars, bottles, tubes, powders, and cakes of all colors are available. Oils, acrylics, and watercolors can all be used in connection with lettering. A stroll through your art supply store will show you all these color possibilities, and maybe even others.

For use with calligraphy, however, the choices

Fig. 8-11. Exercise 79: add serifs before you illuminate.

Fig. 8-12. Exercise 80: draw the illuminated outlines freehand.

can be narrowed. Color that can be used with both paint brush and calligraphy pen is a good choice; this eliminates oils and acrylics as well as plastic paints.

Inks and watercolors seem to be the best choices for adding color to calligraphy. Ink's fluidity works well with both pen and brush, and the colors are vivid. Pelikan, Higgins, and Winsor and Newton

ABCDE FGHIJ KLMN OPQR STUV WXYZ

Fig. 8-13. Exercise 81: now illuminate your alphabet.

all manufacture good-quality colored inks that can be purchased as single bottles or in sets. Colored ink is not meant for illustrating. It will not create an even color in large areas.

Several types of watercolors can be successfully used in calligraphy. Transparent watercolors are thinned until very watery and work better with a brush than with a pen.

Concentrated watercolors are highly concentrated colors that require only a few drops of color for several brushfuls of water. The colors are not permanent, but they are very intense. Luma is a brand of concentrated watercolors that can be used as you would use colored inks.

Designer's colors are designed to fully cover a surface on which they are used. The colors are brilliant and opaque. They can be thinned to transparency. Pelikan, Grumbacher, and Winsor and Newton all produce quality lines of these fairly permanent paints in jars, tubes, or cakes.

The color used most often for the majority of a calligraphy text is still black. It is the most readable and creates a good contrast to calligraphy paper, which is generally white, tan, beige, or ivory.

Early in your calligraphy career it is best to limit your use of color in the text to one color other than black. A traditional color, which dates back to earliest Egyptian history, is vermillion, a red-orange color. The color is made from Mercuric sulfide and is still appropriate on most calligraphy projects. It would be a good choice to use with your mostly black text.

As your calligraphic ability and confidence grow, you can happily experiment with other colors, but always remember to use restraint. Calligraphy is a dignified art that should retain its elegance and simplicity.

When planning a project for reproduction, you must check with your printer to learn his capability to handle certain colors. Your use of color is restricted by his ability to accurately reproduce the color.

When you have created your first piece of calligraphy with a color other than black, take the time to carefully scrutinize the results. Again, be objective and critical, but not harsh.

CORRECTING MISTAKES

Mistakes when applying ink to paper happen to all calligraphers, no matter how expert and experienced they are. In some cases it is most efficient to discard the piece and begin again, but in many instances the work can be saved.

Mistakes in original calligraphy that is to be reproduced can be corrected with the use of Liquid Paper, a standard typist's correction fluid. A letter or word can be covered with the fluid and then relettered. If it is done neatly and carefully, the correction will not show at all when the piece is reproduced by a printer. For the correction of small details white correction fluid applied with a small watercolor brush, works well.

Sometimes fountain-pen ink can be removed from the paper with an ink eradication kit. This kit includes bleach and a neutralizer to stop the action of the bleach. It can only be used in an area where you do not plan to reletter because the ink will blot and spread.

India ink, and once in a while fountain-pen ink, can usually be removed with an abrasive eraser. An Eberhard Faber Pink Pearl eraser or a pencil-end eraser will remove the ink, especially on sturdy papers. India ink will erase more easily than fountain-pen ink since India ink does not soak into the paper.

Another good correction technique for India ink is to very carefully shave off the top layer of the paper along with the mistake. It takes a light touch to successfully make such a correction, but it is a very useful technique to learn. An X-acto utility knife with a #16 blade works well.

Some mistakes can be corrected even more easily. When you do make a mistake, stop and analyze it. You may be able to correct it by simply altering one or more strokes. In other cases, an error may be too serious to correct. It is discouraging to begin all over, but the end result will be worthwhile. Errors too large to be corrected include spacing difficulties and other layout problems.

If layout problems occur regularly in your calligraphy, the problem is probably in the planning. You need to take more time with your rough drafts. Your final layout for a piece of calligraphy should reflect accurately what the finished piece will look like. If you find that your finished piece does not look like the final layout you need to determine why it is so different. Is your layout not complete? Are you changing the plans while executing the piece of artwork?

If you are having difficulty with the transition from final layout to finished product, return to Chapter 7 and go through the step-by-step process of creating a piece of calligraphy. Choose a new project and follow it through from concept to finished product. To make it interesting, and to learn more, choose a very different project from the one you created your first time through the chapter.

It takes a lot of time and patient practice to learn calligraphy, but that practice can and should be fun. The steps to learning are easy if you take them slowly and learn each step thoroughly before moving ahead.

YOU ARE A CALLIGRAPHER

You have learned to write in an entirely new way. By this time Italic handwriting should come fairly easily to your hand. Roman Capitals are also within your capabilities. You know the steps to conceiving, planning, and creating calligraphy as an art form.

Continue to practice regularly and to learn new techniques, but also put your skills on public display now. Show off your calligraphy projects. Don't use your talents only in everyday correspondence and practice. Others will enjoy seeing your efforts, and you may convert a friend or acquaintance into a calligraphy lover and student.

If you have not already done so, offer your services as a calligrapher to an organization, school, or to your friends. Soon you may find that you are being paid to continue with your hobby.

FINDING YOUR OWN STYLE

Calligraphy is a highly individualized art form. You have experimented by now with several lettering variations. Use those that best fit your own personality and the work that you have in progress.

Keep an open mind and never be afraid to try a new style or variation. Design your own unique system of handwriting. Remember, however, that your lettering should always be readable. Don't sacrifice legibility for ornateness.

As suggested earlier, study master calligraphers for clues and insights into ways to improve your writing. Now that your own skills have advanced, you will learn even more with this study. Your eyes will observe more details, and you will better understand how certain appearances and illusions are achieved.

Many texts about calligraphy are available. Now that you have a basic understanding of the subject, you can analyze those books and decide which might be most appropriate for your own calligraphy talents and goals. You may wish to further refine and extend your Italic handwriting, or you may wish to study another style, such as Gothic,

Carolingian, Celtic, Bookhand, or a less well-known specialized hand, such as Dover (Figs. 8-14 through 8-23).

You may also feel the need of an experienced teacher to critique your work now. Enroll in a calligraphy class and share your interest with others.

You can also quit your studies and just concentrate on your Italic writing. It is versatile and will serve all your writing needs.

Calligraphy is also a highly developed art form.

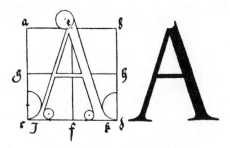

Fig. 8-14. A Dover letter A.

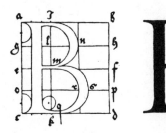

Fig. 8-15. A Dover letter B.

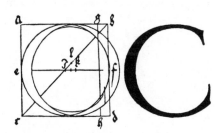

Fig. 8-16. A Dover letter C.

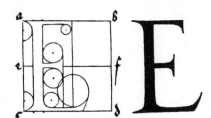

Fig. 8-17. A Dover letter E.

Fig. 8-18. A Dover letter K.

Fig. 8-19. A Dover letter M.

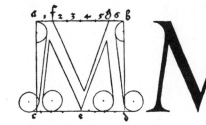

Fig. 8-20. A Dover letter Q.

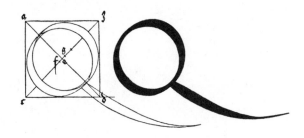

Fig. 8-21. A Dover letter R.

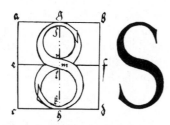

Fig. 8-22. A Dover letter S.

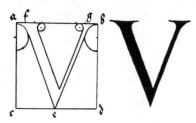

Fig. 8-23. A Dover letter V.

The choice is yours. Your calligraphy can simply be a hobby that improved your handwriting; it can be a very personal art; it can be a part-time job with good pay, or it can be a lucrative full-time business.

Chapter 9 will tell you how to turn calligraphy into a business. Just as it is easy and inexpensive to learn calligraphy, it is easy and inexpensive to launch a business based on calligraphy.

The tools and materials you will need for a professional calligraphy studio will be presented; the location and design of the studio will be discussed, and ways of advertising will be explored. The printing process will be briefly examined, along with how to prepare originals for reproduction. You can find out how to price your services, and how to serve potential customers and their needs.

9.
Calligraphy
As a Business

A serious calligrapher can earn a full-time income with a freelance business based in your home. The investment is small, and the business can grow gradually as orders become more frequent.

Many calligraphers find themselves with a small side income without even trying. As word circulates that you are becoming an accomplished calligrapher, you are likely to begin getting inquiries on producing calligraphy for pay. The possibilities for establishing a calligraphy business are greatly varied.

If you seek a part-time income that will support your calligraphy hobby, consider creating and framing a number of quotations and poems and selling them at local craft bazaars. Of course you can always take special orders at the bazaar to fill later. By appearing at a bazaar with your pieces of art, you are also becoming known as a local calligrapher. At your table, hand out business cards for future contacts. Later, if you decide to expand your business, you will have the income from the bazaars

with which to begin advertising and to purchase the tools and materials you will need for a professional calligraphy studio.

Calligraphy as a business has many advantages for the independent craftsman. Your talents will grow rapidly as you perform a variety of tasks; you will be earning money doing something that is pleasurable, and you will be able to work in your own home or at location of your choice.

On the other hand, starting any small business is risky. The monetary investment and the investment of your personal effort could be lost. The business could also survive, but only a shoestring. It can take several years for any business to become established and lucrative.

It can be done successfully, however. The safest way to begin is to begin on a small scale. Don't give up your other source of income until the calligraphy business grows to the point where it demands the majority of your time and efforts, and is providing a steady income.

WHAT PROJECTS CAN YOU SELL?

All of the calligraphy projects that have been mentioned throughout this book can be sold. Poetry, quotations, invitations, greeting cards (Fig. 9-1), placecards, and name tags can be potential orders. Many businesses and organizations also need programs, advertisements, signs, letterheads, menus, business cards, awards (Fig. 9-2), po'sters (Fig. 9-3), envelopes, labels, book or album jackets, and packaging.

Look around you during the day, and you will discover many more ideas. Once your services are known, customers will bring you ideas.

Design your business to fit your needs and talents. Take on jobs that will stretch your skills and imagination, making you grow. Don't attempt to tackle jobs that are beyond your capabilities, however. Perhaps you can work out an arrangement with an established, expert calligrapher in your area where you handle his routine, overflow work, and he or she takes over the jobs that are too intricate for your still-growing talents.

The same arrangement can be used with art that is needed on calligraphy. If you are not an expert artist, call on one when original artwork is required on a piece of commissioned calligraphy. In turn you can furnish calligraphy when the artist is in need of lettering.

Be flexible. Tailor your business to fit the calligraphy needs of your community. If the needs are minimal, keep your business small. If the needs are great, take advantage and let your business grow. Consider a partnership with another free-lancer, or with an artist, or share office space with an artist or other compatible service. The ways of setting up your business are endless. A thorough

Fig. 9-1. A professionally designed calligraphy greeting card.

OREGON COLUMBIA   IABC

Award of Merit

IABC   OREGON CASCADE

Dick Baltus
RECIPIENT

Oregon Health Sciences Center
COMPANY

One Person Projects-Newspapers
CATEGORY

PRESIDENT

May 13, 1983
DATE

Fig. 9-2. Awards can be your greatest business.

analysis of the calligraphy needs of your area is critical; it will determine the scope of your business. Careful planning can mean the difference between the success or failure of your business.

CALLIGRAPHY IS A NEEDED SERVICE

There is a need for calligraphy. Look around and see all the ways that calligraphy is used every day. The jacket of a book you pick up to read may be designed in calligraphy. Billboards and advertisements often are lettered in a calligraphy style. A letter you receive in the mail may have a letterhead originated by a calligrapher. The business card a salesman hands you may be done in calligraphy. The list could go on. Promotional buttons often carry calligraphy. Fabric and wooden wall hangings sometimes have messages written in calligraphy.

At some point a calligrapher was paid for initiating each of those products. Sometimes a calligraphy job can be the creation of one unique item. Other times a job may consist of readying an original for reproduction thousands of times, or a job may consist of producing 10, 20, or 100 originals. One advantage of a career in calligraphy is the true variety of tasks.

Perhaps by now you have decided to turn your

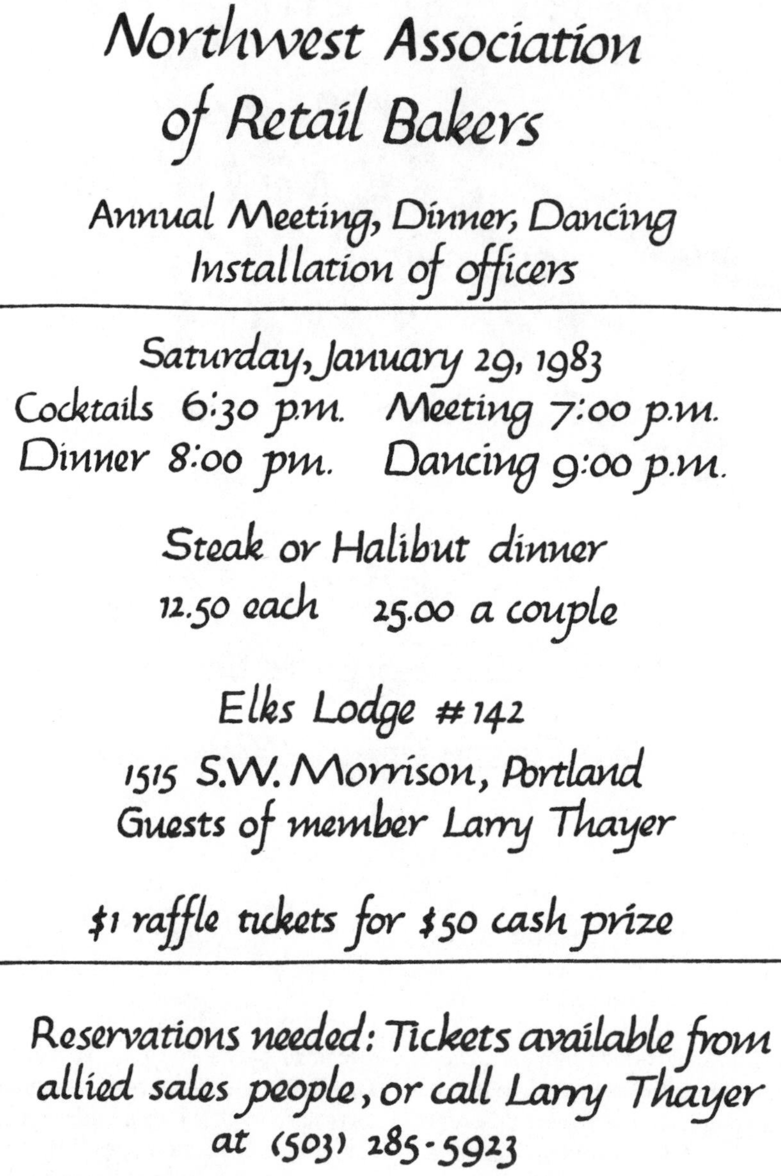

Northwest Association
of Retail Bakers

Annual Meeting, Dinner, Dancing
Installation of officers

Saturday, January 29, 1983
Cocktails 6:30 p.m. Meeting 7:00 p.m.
Dinner 8:00 pm. Dancing 9:00 p.m.

Steak or Halibut dinner
12.50 each   25.00 a couple

Elks Lodge #142
1515 S.W. Morrison, Portland
Guests of member Larry Thayer

$1 raffle tickets for $50 cash prize

Reservations needed: Tickets available from
allied sales people, or call Larry Thayer
at (503) 285-5923

Fig. 9-3. A poster done entirely in calligraphy.

hobby into a real business. Selling at bazaars and through a classified ad can support your calligraphy hobby and even bring in a small income, but it takes more to earn a living at your craft. You have the opportunity to pursue a career in calligraphy in several different ways.

In order to turn calligraphy into a full-time freelance business you must first of all extend your research into the calligraphy market in your locale.

RESEARCHING THE MARKET PLACE

One of your best sources of information will probably be other freelance calligraphers. Talk with several who are in your part of the country but far enough away so that they will feel comfortable giving you detailed information. A calligrapher who will be in competition with you for business is going to be unwilling to divulge much helpful information.

Ask the freelancers questions about the beginning of their business. Why did they begin a freelance calligraphy business? How long have they been in business? How much capital did they put into the business? When did they begin to see a profit? Do they earn a full-time living? What percentage of their income is profit? How do they price their work? How many hours a week do they work? Do they barter some of their services? Do they work with an artist on some jobs? If they do work with an artist, how is the commission shared? How did they find the best printer in the area? Is the business growing? Is there room for more freelance calligraphers? What have they found to be the most effective advertising?

The more questions you ask, the better prepared you will be for opening your own business. What kind of record-keeping system do they use? How are clients billed? What supplies and tools do they recommend for a beginning freelancer? What do they predict for the future of their business?

Prepare for your interviews as if you were an investigative reporter. Write down all of your questions beforehand, but don't intimidate your sources of information with an onslaught of questions like an interrogator. Keep it casual, but get the most information you can. It would be a good investment to buy lunch for your fellow freelancer. Many valuable tidbits of information and business ideas are shared over lunch.

In addition to interviewing several freelance calligraphers in person, you can write letters. If your sources of information are too far from your base of operations, a friendly letter might elicit some helpful comments.

Other sources of information will give you different points of view. Suppliers of calligraphy materials and tools may have a good overview of what is happening in the field in your part of the country. They should know which cities and towns purchase the most calligraphy supplies. They also may have valuable contacts with people in related busi-nesses. Get from them any price lists available, and ask about discounts.

People who teach calligraphy in your area also have a great deal of inside information about the field. They may even sell some of their calligraphy on a freelance basis also, but since it is not a full-time business they may be willing to share their knowledge. They will know of suppliers, other calligraphers, and the local market, and they probably have many suggestions concerning the implementation of your business.

Talk also with local artists, writers, calligraphy clubs, and related associations. Ask for copies of club newsletters.

You will be gathering as much information as possible about calligraphy and making a living as a freelance calligrapher.

After talking with all of the people associated with calligraphy, there are still other people who can be extremely helpful in the planning stages of your career. Interview all of the local printers; you will probably need printing services early in your career, when a customer orders invitations, business cards, or other reproducible items. Some questions to ask printers are suggested later in this chapter, along with explanations of the printing processes.

Preliminary contacts with prospective clients can also be useful now. Advertising agencies and publishers may be among your major clients. Talk to their representatives in the nearest city in your area. They will be able to tell you if and when they use freelance calligraphers, and on what types of projects. Contact the local newspaper about designing and/or lettering some of their advertisements. Call on local businesses, asking about the potential for business cards, letterheads, fliers, advertising supplements, signs, window displays, and other calligraphy needs.

Visit your library or bookstore for books on how to start a small business. There are many excellent manuals available. Read several, or parts of several, and glean out the pertinent information.

After you have gathered all of the information about the local calligraphy market, freelance calligraphy, and beginning a small business, take some time to assimilate all of the data. Read it, take notes, organize the data, and make a notebook or folder about your potential freelance calligraphy business. It could be the start of a new way of life for you.

DEVELOPING THE NEED

You know the value of calligraphy. You know where and how it can be used. You know how calligraphy can be used to enhance advertising, correspondence, information, and almost any written communication.

Educating Clients

In order to make your calligraphy business profitable, you must educate your potential clients to the benefits of calligraphy. You must confidently show your community how you can help them in many different ways. You must show businessmen and individuals that they have a need for calligraphy, and you must convince them that you are the person to fill that need. You will need to accomplish this objective in several simultaneous ways.

You need to convince those potential customers that calligraphy is the right medium for their message, and you must make them realize that you are the right artist to fill the assignment. Many future customers will see your work at bazaars or other places where it may be displayed. Any time you hang a piece of calligraphy where it will be seen by potential customers, be sure it is signed. If possible, have business cards nearby so that someone in need of calligraphy can get in touch with you easily.

Since displaying your work is one of the best advertisements for calligraphy, you can make up a variety of samples, similar to an artist or photographer's portfolio, which a businessman can study, and which may give him new ideas of ways he can use calligraphy.

You can also take several pieces from the portfolio and design a flyer to distribute through direct mail advertising. Some prospective clients may warrant a specific portfolio done about their company, including business cards for the president, company letterhead and envelope design,

window posters, and sample advertisements for newspaper or magazines.

Setting the Scope of Your Business

You must also make another decision. You must determine the scope of your business. Do you intend to limit your business to simply lettering exactly what a client directs, or will you also act as an artistic consultant, advising a client on his calligraphy needs? Can you design advertisements?

Set the parameters of your business before you begin accepting assignments. It is much better for your business image for you to decline an assignment than for you to have to return it to a client unfinished after two or three weeks. This is where it can be a real advantage to work closely with a more advanced calligrapher, so that between you both, you can probably accept every project that is offered.

To make it easy for a customer to have access to your services, offer to make a presentation in his or her office. This presentation can be an advantage to you in that you will get the feel and flavor of the operation to which you are attempting to sell your services as a calligrapher.

Other Potential Customers

In addition to local individuals and businesses, there are many other contacts you can make for customers and referrals to potential customers. Trade associations often host conventions, offer certificates of merit, and need membership cards. You can find a list of these associations in local telephone books. Send them a package with samples of your work, along with a personal letter suggesting ways in which they can use your talents.

Contact all local publishers, and even regional publishers if you are willing to travel some for your business. Most or all of the business for a client 150 or even 1,000, miles away may be able to be handled by mail. Nearly all newspaper and magazine publishers are supported by advertising, which must be designed and originated by an expert. In some cases a calligrapher may be the best choice for an ad designer. You may be able to set up a regular schedule with a publisher to do a certain amount of

Fig. 9-4. Assorted colored inks.

Fig. 9-5. Spray finishes for professional calligraphy projects.

his advertising, or you may be on call to supplemnnt regular staff when necessary.

Advertising agencies also design and produce ads of all types for a great variety of clients. The majority of their ads may be commercially typeset, but for an occasional account they may need the elegance of calligraphy. If the agency has a portfolio of your work on file, you may be the calligrapher they call.

These contacts with trade associations, publishers, and advertising agencies can lead to offers of full-time employment, or they can lead to a few regular clients who produce enough business to keep you busy full time as a freelance calligrapher, setting your own hours and working from your own location.

Setting your own hours, however, doesn't mean that you only have to work when you feel like it. To be a successful small business manager or freelancer, you need to keep fairly regular hours, but don't be afraid to bend the rules to suit your family at times. That's another of the advantages of being a self-employed artist.

FILLING THE NEEDS OF YOUR COMMUNITY

Your research and the early months of your calligraphy business will tell you a great deal. Most of all you will learn what the needs of the area are for calligraphy, and you will know how well equipped you are to meet those needs.

Improving Skills

You will learn in what areas you need to extend your knowledge and skills to meet those needs. Additional practice of your present skills is of course helpful. You may wish, however, to tackle other styles of calligraphy, either through advanced calligraphy books, or through classes with expert calligraphers.

You may also decide that a class in advertising would be beneficial. Classes are offered in advertising layout as well as in selling advertising. Classes in small business management or in accounting may be helpful in making your operation run more smoothly.

There is always a way to improve. If you are constantly striving to improve, your business should not only survive, it should prosper.

Keeping Customers

You have become a professional calligrapher. You deserve the respect that every artist should receive. You have established a business and are busy filling orders. You've got those first orders, but it's very important to ensure that those customers return.

Make It Easy for Them to Return. Be sure that they have your name and telephone number. It should be prominent on your business cards, letterheads, and invoices. If feasible, offer a pick-up and delivery service on all orders. Offer an extra bonus with orders; it should be simple and inexpensive, but it should remind them of you and the quality of your work—perhaps a sign, plaque, or name card. Regular, satisfied customers are the heart of your business.

Be Flexible. The needs of the community and your own talents will determine the direction that your freelance calligraphy business will take. As your business grows, allow it to mature naturally; that way it will reach a comfortable compromise between the calligraphy needs of the area and your own talents and future aspirations.

THE PROFESSIONAL CALLIGRAPHY STUDIO

The well-equipped studio will house a variety of pens to suit the talents of the calligrapher and the needs of the clientele. A variety of inks and paints will also be necessary. Begin with a few standard basics and add more as they become necessary. Among your inks will probably be Higgins Waterproof Ink, Higgins General Drawing Ink, India Ink, and a Chinese inkstick with an inkstone. A few good colored inks will also be needed (Fig. 9-4).

Other materials that every professional calligraphy studio should contain include: pencils, erasers, a t-square, pencil sharpener, an erasing shield, pen cleaner, storage unit for materials and finished art work, frames, razor blades or a utility knife, brushes, rulers, masking tape, spray finishes, rubber cement and thinner (Fig. 9-5).

The studio will need to offer a variety of good paper as discussed in Chapter 7. Again, begin with a limited supply and add more as necessary.

You can establish your business with a drawing board and graduate later to a drafting table. The drawing board should be at least 20 × 26 inches, with a true edge on the left side. Also available is a portable drafting table, which has the advantage of being a permanent table on a stable base. It should also have a true edge as well as a retaining strip at the bottom edge. It can be constructed of metal, wood, or plastic. The table top should be protected from scratches with a vinyl sheet, which is available at art supply stores.

A comfortable chair that allows the calligrapher to work easily at the drafting table is vital. Good lighting is required in your calligraphy studio. When possible, take advantage of the natural morning light. When natural light is not available, use a combination of incandescent and fluorescent lighting to create the light most nearly imitating natural sunlight. It is more expensive than either incandescent of fluorescent alone, which are both acceptable. Most important is that no glare reflect off the working paper.

All of your tools and materials must be kept scrupulously clean, or your finished products will have smudges that seriously detract from the appearance.

MONEY MATTERS

Naturally you are concerned about the cost of starting your freelance calligraphy business. The amount of investment will be dictated by your financial assets and needs, as well as your plans and goals for the business. There is no set formula.

The investment of a few dollars in materials and tools, along with the price of renting a table or booth at a few local bazaars, is enough to get some calligraphers set up in business. Others, due to different goals and talents, as well as capital availability, may initially plunge hundreds or even thousands of dollars into the business.

While one calligrapher may begin making bazaar items in a vacant corner at home, another may rent a downtown studio or office in which to set up shop. Individuality, as in all other phases of calligraphy, determines how and where the business will be set up. No matter how small or large you envision your business, however, accurate record keeping is a must.

For tax purposes, as well as for income determination, records must be kept. All orders should be in writing and the customer and the calligrapher should each keep a copy. The order form should include details about the item ordered, number requested, customer's name, address and telephone number, and the estimated price. All payments made to or from the business should also be recorded. At tax time it will then be easy to do the required paperwork or have it done by a professional tax preparer.

Setting the fees for your service is difficult. It is another area where a freelance calligrapher in a noncompetitive location can supply much valuable information. The cost of materials, your time and expertise, the difficulty of the job, and the size of the job all must be considered when you quote a price.

Prices are different for one piece of original work, a quantity of originals, and one original and printed reproductions. As with setting up your business, there is no set formula to tell you how much to charge for your services. Most beginning calligraphers tend to price their services too low, but as their confidence and abilities progress, their prices are adjusted to reflect that growth.

Some jobs will consist of one original piece of calligraphy. Some jobs will include artwork for which you may need to hire an artist. Some jobs will require the services of a print shop. When these cases occur, and you are responsible for the total job, add a service charge for handling the entire project.

There is one last money matter that must be considered—advertising. The best advertising is word of mouth. Tell your friends what you are doing. Tell your local calligrapher's group that you are ready to do some calligraphy for pay.

Another effective way of getting the word out is with letters, in calligraphy of course, to local businesses and organizations who might be possible clients. You can make one original and have it reproduced inexpensively at a print shop.

The classified section of your newspaper is a good place to list your new business. Also consider the yellow pages of the telephone book.

Make up some fliers or posters promoting your business and post them on local bulletin boards. Also call people who you think are potential clients. To come up with more ways of advertising, analyze your community for possible customers and determine how you can most inexpensively reach them with the information that you are now in business.

THE PRINTING PROCESS

The very best way to learn about printing is to visit all of the local print shops. Talk to the manager, ask about his machines, and ask for samples of what the machine will do. Find out what papers are available and if any others can be specially ordered. Ask about prices; get a price list if possible. Is there a discount for repeat customers? What colored inks are available? How long will it take to have an order filled?

Carefully examine any samples you get. Is the printing clear and crisp? Is it clean? Are the colors bright or faded? Also notice the condition of the shop. Any print shop will have stacks of paper around and a certain amount of clutter, but if the shop is truly dirty, chances are your orders will come back smudged and dirty.

Also pay attention to the manager's attitude. Hopefully you will be working with the manager often; so a compatible relationship is desirable.

The method of printing for calligraphy used most often is offset lithography. It is readily available and relatively inexpensive, and the quality is excellent. Most quick print shops offer offset lithography printing, and these shops can be found in all metropolitan areas and even most small towns.

In offset lithography, the camera-ready page is photographed, and an aluminum, stainless steel, or paper plate is made of the image. The image from the plate is then transferred to a rubber "blanket" cylinder, which prints the image onto the paper.

Two other forms of printing are sometimes indicated. One is gravure. Gravure is well suited for very large quantities because the quality can be controlled more consistently. *Gravure* is a form of etching that began in the fifteenth century. A gravure plate is etched, and ink is then applied to the plate surface. A scraper is then used to remove any ink except that which is in the recessed areas of the plate. The image on the paper is then formed when the pressure of a large cylinder causes the ink to be drawn from the recessed areas.

The third printing process is called letterpress. One advantage of letterpress is that it can be used with embossing. *Letterpress,* or relief, printing is the oldest of the three printing methods generally used. To make a plate for letterpress printing, a photographic negative is made of the original art. The negative is placed on a metal plate and exposed to light. The light hardens the exposed surfaces, and the unexposed areas are eliminated in an acid bath, leaving just the image areas raised slightly above the plate's surface. This raised part of the plate then receives the ink and transfers the image to paper.

Look at each job you receive individually and determine the best method of printing for each. As your business grows, and you work with printing, you will learn exactly what local printers can accomplish, and you will learn how to best prepare copy and artwork for each printer.

At times you will need to have artwork or your calligraphy copy enlarged or reduced. Many print shops have the machinery to do such work. Remember, however, that any enlargement or reduction will be proportional; that is, the entire piece that is being changed will differ both horizontally and vertically by the same percentage.

Check with your local printers about how to do color separations. When more than one color is called for in printing, each color must be done separately. Each printer will tell you how color jobs are handled in his shop.

TEACHING CALLIGRAPHY

Another way of earning money using calligraphy is by sharing your talent. Calligraphy is taught in many art centers and community schools.

YMCA and YWCA chapters offer a variety of classes, and they may like to add calligraphy to their course offerings. Perhaps a museum in your area hosts classes. Check your library, telephone book, and chamber of commerce for ideas about where to offer your services as a calligraphy teacher. You could also set aside a room in your home, or use your calligraphy studio, as a classroom. Advertise in the classified section and begin your own calligraphy lessons in your home.

Until your calligraphy skills reach the expert level, limit your instruction to beginning classes. Italics is the most common form of calligraphy used today and can be useful to people in many ways. Beginners may wish only to improve their everyday handwriting, or they may take your class as a first step toward becoming a professional calligrapher.

Keep your lessons simple and direct, and constantly encourage your students to practice faithfully. Remember that your students are beginners who need a lot of praise and encouragement. Keep criticism gentle and constructive.

YOUR OWN CALLIGRAPHY

Whether you choose to launch a career teaching calligraphy, set up your studio and go into the freelance calligraphy business, or limit your calligraphy to personal use, you have acquired a useful new talent. Use it.

Calligraphy can be a creative, enjoyable, beautiful way of expressing your thoughts and ideas. Make it your own art. Now that you know the basic rules of calligraphy, experiment until you have a truly individual form of handwriting. *Calligraphy* means beautiful writing. Through a series of easy steps, you now have beautiful writing at your command.

Glossary

acrylics—Plastic paints in which pigments are dispersed in an acrylic emulsion. They do not work well for calligraphy.

ascender—The part of the letter that rises above the body.

asymmetrical—Nonsymmetrical. The two halves are not the same.

base line—The line on which the body of most letters rests.

blackletter—The dense, compact Gothic style of writing.

body—The portion of a letter that is contained between two guidelines.

bookhand—A style of writing based on ancient manuscripts done in Carolingian.

broad-edge—Pen nibs with a flat edge like a chisel.

built-up letters—Letters that have been widened by adding extra strokes. Filled in built-up letters become illuminated letters.

burnisher—A hand tool with an agate tip that is used to polish gold leaf.

calligraphy—The art of beautiful writing.

Carolingian—The first alphabet to use true minuscule letters with ascenders and descenders. It was discovered in France and promoted by Charlemagne.

centered—Symmetrically balanced.

Chancery Cursive—An ornate form of the Italic alphabet which is featured in this book. It originated during the fifteenth century.

chamois—Smooth, clean doeskin. Often used for wiping calligraphy pens.

chisel point—Another term for broad edge, which means a pen nib with a flat edge like a chisel.

cipher—Letters that are interlaced to create a design for identification or ornamentation of personal items.

Copperplate—Writing style from the eighteenth century when pointed nibs were first used by scribes to copy the fine lines made by an engraver's burin.

counters—Spaces within letters that are used to correctly form and proportion letters.

Cursive—Writing that is formed rapidly with joined letters.

deckle—A frayed edge on handmade paper. It is caused by the frame that holds the paper.

descender—The part of the letter that falls below the bottom guideline.

designers' colors—Opaque water colors that are well suited for calligraphy.

dipping—The way in which nibs are filled with ink.

draftsman's pencil—Mechanical pencil with a slip-proof knurled grip.

drawing pen—A special pen for drawing very fine lines.

dry cleaner—Powdered cleaner in a cloth pouch. It is used for cleaning large areas of paper, and for roughening very smooth paper surfaces.

elbow nib—A specially designed pen with a bend in the shaft. It is used for writing in the Copperplate style.

filler—Design drawn with a pen to fill blank spaces in the text.

final draft—A complete plan for the finished manuscript.

finisher—A stroke that extends from the last letter at the end of a line or paragraph and used to decorate the open area.

flourish—Decoration of letters, usually achieved by adding sweeping strokes.

flush—Handlettered or typeset lines with one margin of the text even along the edge.

format—General design, shape, content, or size, such as a newspaper format.

French curve—A plastic or metal drafting tool that is used to draw arcs or ovals.

gild—To illuminate a manuscript with gold leaf, or with gold leaf and colors.

Gothic—A general style of writing that became popular early in the twelfth century. Majuscule letters designed to be used only with minuscules also appeared during this time.

grain—The direction of the fibers in a piece of paper. There is usually a dominant grain in machine-made paper but not in handmade paper.

guidelines—The lines that set the vertical boundaries of a letter. They can be real, such as the lines on your practice notebook or graph paper, or penciled-in or imaginary lines.

hairlines—Fine lines, most often used with Blackletter, at the end of a stroke.

half-Uncial—A style of lettering that preceded the Carolingian. It looks like a minuscule alphabet but is not.

heading—A title for a manuscript. It is usually emphasized in some manner.

hone—To sharpen.

Humanist—A period in history when scholars attempted to regain some of the cultural excellence of ancient Rome.

Illumination—A method of decorating the text of a manuscript with gold, silver, and colors.

interlinear spacing—The amount of space between lines of writing.

Italic—Writing that is slanted. It is also the name of the specific form of calligraphy that is most popular today.

join—The line connecting two letters.

justify—To adjust the space between words so that lines of lettering or type fit the allotted space and are even at both margins.

kid—The surface texture of bristol board of medium tooth. It is very popular with calligraphers.

layout—The overall design of a page.

leading—In typography, the amount of space between lines of type.

letter familes—Groups of letters that share characteristics.

letterpress—A printing process in which the plate image to be inked is above the surface of the plate.

logotype (logo)—Letters combined into a symbolic design.

majuscules—Capital letters.

manuscript—A book or document done in handwriting.

minuscules—Lowercase letters.

monogram—Two or more letters combined in a design in which one letter forms part of another.

nib—The part of the pen that draws ink from the reservoir to the point. It is also the actual point of the pen.

nibbing—Making a nib from a reed or quill.

opaque—Impenetrable by light; too dense to be seen through.

offset lithography—A printing method where the inked image is on the same plane as the plate.

ornamentation—Anything that is used to beautify a letter, word, or manuscript.

overlay—A sheet of transparent paper or film that is placed over artwork to protect it and indicate instructions.

Palmer—A method of penmanship instruction using the Copperplate hand script form.

papyrus—Writing material used by the ancient Egyptians, Greeks, and Romans and made from the pith of a sedgelike plant native to the Nile region.

parallel rule—A drafting instrument that is attached to a drafting board and which consists of a single straightedge riding on a track of wire or waxed twine and used in place of a t-square.

parchment—Writing material that is made from the skin of a goat or sheep.

pen angle—The angle made by the flat end of the pen and the horizontal guideline.

pen width—The width of the writing edge on a broad-edge pen drawn at a perfect vertical; used as a standard measuring device to establish proportions between ascender, descender, and body.

pointed nib—A steel pen nib with a single slit at its point; found on common fountain pens as well as the elbow nib and crow-quill pens used for copperplate.

Practical Italics—A calligraphy style of lettering that features oval letters with long ascenders and descenders, with a slight right-hand slant. It is one of the styles taught in this book and is suitable for everyday use.

printing plate—The surface carrying the inked image that is transferred directly to paper or, as in offset lithography, to a rubber blanket that transfers the image to the paper.

proportion—The ratio between parts of a letter.

rag content—The amount of linen or cotton rags used in making high-quality papers; most common papers are made of wood pulp.

ragged—The arrangement of lines of type or lettering so that either the right or left margin is uneven.

ream—The amount of paper of any dimension, usually 480 to 500 sheets.

reed—A tubular plant stock that can be used to make a crude pen.

reservoir—The permanent or removable device that is attached to a pen's nib and holds the ink or paint.

Roundhand—Another term for Copperplate used because of its rounded strokes.

rubricate—To use the color red when writing on a manuscript, especially on illuminated pages.

ruling pen—A drafting instrument used for drawing lines of varying degrees of thickness with the assistance of a straightedge.

Rustica—A letterform using a very steep pen angle; preceded the Uncial alphabet.

sable—Hair used in the finest watercolor brushes.

scaling—Determining the percentage of enlargement or reduction of artwork by using a scaling wheel or geometric proportions.

scrivener—A professional penman, scribe, copyist, clerk, or secretary.

scroll—Normally a document that has been prepared by a professional scribe or scrivener and usually rolled up when presented or stored.

serifs—Small, decorative strokes placed on open ends of basic letters.

shades—Copperplate strokes with both a thickness and a squared-off end.

spacing—The distance between letters.

stylus—A pointed instrument used to impress a drawing into a surface.

swash—A separate, decorative pen stroke added to the basic form of the letter.

swells—Copperplate strokes that begin and end as hairlines, with a tapering bulge in the middle of the body.

tempera—A common term for opaque water colors and poster colors.

Textura—Blackletter.

transparent—Any medium capable of transmitting light, such as transparent watercolors.

triangle—A metal or plastic instrument used with a t-square to draw vertical and diagonal lines.

true edge—A metal strip attached to a drawing board and used to assist the t-square in smooth and accurate movement.

t-square—A drafting device that can be used in calligraphy to accurately draw horizontal lines.

typography—The composition, arrangement, and design of printed matter from movable type.

Uncial—A majuscule letterform found in Greek and Latin manuscripts deriving its name from the Roman *uncia* or inch.

value—The degree of darkness or lightness in color.

vellum—A writing material made from the skins of lambs, kids, or calfs.

vermillion—A red pigment found on ancient Egyptian manuscripts and made from mercuric sulfide. It was popular on medieval manuscripts. Today, it can be duplicated by cadmium red light.

versal—A letterform deriving its name and characteristics from the first letter of a verse which is enlarged and decorated.

waist line—The line that corresponds to the center of a letter or to the top of a minuscule.

waterproof—Inks that are resistant to water after they dry, though not necessarily permanent.

watermark—A faint, translucent design impressed into paper that identifies the maker. It can often be read by holding the sheet up to the light.

Index

Edited by Suzanne L. Cheatle

OTHER POPULAR TAB BOOKS OF INTEREST